When You Pray

When You Pray

A Prayer Book for Christians Today

compiled by
John Gilling and Madeleine Evans

Foreword by
Rt Revd Graham Leonard

Darton, Longman and Todd
London

First published in 1978 by
Darton, Longman & Todd Ltd
89 Lillie Road, London SW6 1UD

Reprinted 1979 and 1981
Revised edition 1987
Revised edition reprinted 1989 and 1992

British Library Cataloguing in Publication Data

When you pray: a prayer book for
    Christians today.—Rev. ed.
    1. Church of England—Prayer-books and
    devotions.
    I. Gilling, John   II. Evans, Madeleine
    242′.803   BX5145

ISBN 0–232–51711–8

Phototypeset by Input Typesetting Ltd
Printed and bound in Great Britain by
Courier International Ltd,
East Kilbride, Scotland

Acknowledgement

The compilers wish to thank Elizabeth Russell and
Ann Douglas for their help in producing this new
edition.

Contents

Foreword

When we are baptised into Christ we are also made members of the great company of the faithful, the majority of whom are already beyond the grave. It is with all the saints that we shall come to know the greatness of the love of God.

As we live on earth and seek to express the relationship which God has given us to himself in Christ by our prayers, we can and should draw upon the experience of the great servants of God throughout the centuries. In this way, as we pray, our prayers are enabled to grow so that they become more truly the prayer of Christ in us.

This book of prayers for Christians today gives us a splendid framework which, while giving us the discipline we need, also sets us free to grow in prayer. It does so by putting at our disposal the prayers, praise and affirmation of Christians throughout the ages. At a time when it is increasingly difficult to resist the pressure to be conformed to this world in its thinking and priorities we need the help of our brothers and sisters in Christ if we are to be transformed by the renewing of our minds so that we see the glory and beauty of the will of God and be inspired to obey in love.

I was very glad to commend this book when it was first published. What I then wrote has been fully justified by its initial success and by the continuing demand. The publication of a new edition is very welcome, and I am sure that the book will continue to have the popularity which it deserves.

+ GRAHAM LONDIN

How to use this Book

Using a book of prayers is very different from our ordinary reading, starting at the beginning and going on to the end and then stopping. When you first look at this book it is a good idea to read the list of contents and then skim through the book just to see if anything is of particular interest to you. After this it would be natural to read slowly and meditatively those parts of the book which seem to be most useful or interesting, so that these can sink into the mind.

But this book is meant to be prayed rather than read. So before you begin to use it you have to decide whether you really want to pray and how long you wish to spend in prayer each day. Prayer is talking and listening to God: if we do not make up our minds to give a certain amount of time to this, the result will be that we forget him and our lives will lose the richness and depth that they gain by being close to him.

If we can spare only a few minutes each day then the best thing we can do is simply to repeat the 'Prayers commonly used by Christians' every day. These great prayers will at least take us for a few moments into the air of God. If we have a little more time, then it would be best to use one of the sets of 'Daily Prayers' (the first is the shortest) further on in the book as well. If, during the day, we find we have moments when we can spend a minute or two in prayer, then we can use some of the prayers in the section 'Praying round the Clock'.

From time to time, perhaps on Sunday, we may be able to do a little more. So we could usefully spend this time praying for other people (using the section 'Intercessions') or reviewing our own lives (using the section 'Penitence'), even better, in thinking about God (using the section 'Meditation and Contemplation').

If we use the forms of daily prayer regularly we shall probably find they become a rather dull routine. So there are special prayers for each day of the week, the words of which are drawn from the services of the Church and from the Bible, and which commemorate God's acts in Creation and Redemption. These are more difficult to use but they are full of treasures – so full that it may be better to use only a part of them, taking a phrase or two from each part into which they are divided.

If we take this little book to church we can use it at the Eucharist to help us pray as we offer the holy sacrifice and make our communion. There are also prayers to be used when we cannot get to church in the section 'Making a Spiritual Communion'.

The Christian year is divided into different seasons like Lent and Advent, and a few prayers are included which can be used at the appropriate time. There is also a selection of traditional prayers and devotions, many of which have been used by Christians all over the world for centuries, together with some prayers of our own times.

For your own favourite prayers and for prayers you make up yourself, pages 139–44 have been left blank. Some people, who are used to praying always in their own words, may find that the prayers are long and too detailed; others may find that the prayers and the descriptive parts of the book are too brief and too prosaic. But we know from our own experience that if we simply talk to God in our own words we leave out a great deal that we should include. There have, moreover, been times in our lives, the grey times, when we have needed the help that a book like this can provide, because otherwise we should have found it impossible to pray at all.

This book is meant to help us to pray. The prayers are taken from many sources, Roman Catholic and Orthodox as well as Anglican and Free Church. You may find that you would prefer not to use some of them if, for example, you do not like directly addressing the saints in your prayers. In that case simply leave them out. Some of the best prayers of all, the Psalms, have not been included in full because we wished to keep this book as short as possible. You will, of course, find them in the Bible, and anyone who is used to praying will find that as he or she gets older they become more and more a part of prayer. We would like to end with a quotation from one: 'We wish you good luck in the name of the Lord.'

JOHN GILLING
MADELEINE EVANS

LOVE

Love bade me welcome; yet my soul drew back,
      Guilty of dust and sin.
But quick-ey'd Love, observing me grow slack
      From my first entrance in,
Drew nearer to me, sweetly questioning
      If I lack'd any thing.

'A guest,' I answer'd, 'worthy to be here':
      Love said, 'You shall be he.'
'I, the unkind, ungrateful? Ah, my dear,
      I cannot look on Thee.'
Love took my hand, and smiling did reply,
      'Who made the eyes but I?'

'Truth, Lord; but I have marr'd them; let my shame
      Go where it doth deserve.'
'And know you not', says Love, 'Who bore the blame?'
      'My dear, then I will serve.'
'You must sit down,' says Love, 'and taste My meat.'
      So I did sit and eat.

GEORGE HERBERT

Prayers commonly used by Christians

Our Father

Our Father, who art in heaven
Hallowed be thy Name.
Thy Kingdom come.
Thy will be done on earth as it is in heaven.
Give us this day our daily bread,
And forgive us our trespasses
As we forgive those who trespass against us.
Lead us not into temptation
But deliver us from evil,
For thine is the Kingdom, the Power and the Glory
for ever and ever.

Hail Mary

Hail Mary, full of grace
The Lord is with thee.
Blessed art thou among women
And blessed is the fruit of thy womb, Jesus.
Holy Mary, Mother of God,
Pray for us sinners, now and at the hour of our death.

Glory be . . .

Glory be to the Father and to the Son and to the
Holy Spirit
As it was in the beginning is now and ever shall be,
world without end.

I believe . . .

I believe in God, the Father Almighty
Maker of heaven and earth.
And in Jesus Christ, his only Son, our Lord
Who was conceived by the Holy Ghost
Born of the Virgin Mary
Suffered under Pontius Pilate
Was crucified, dead and buried.
He descended into hell;
The third day he rose again from the dead;
He ascended into heaven
And sitteth on the right hand of God the Father
Almighty.
From thence he shall come to judge the quick and
the dead.
I believe in the Holy Ghost; the Holy Catholic
Church;
The Communion of Saints; the forgiveness of sins;
The Resurrection of the body;
And the life everlasting.

The Grace

The grace of our Lord Jesus Christ, the love of God
and the fellowship of the Holy Spirit be with us all
evermore.

Daily Prayer

*It is helpful to have a pattern when we pray. Here are three
sets of prayers based on the same pattern. After recollecting
God's presence with us there follow prayers (of)*

(i) praise
(ii) penitence
(iii) intercession (praying for others)
(iv) petition (praying for oneself)
(v) thanksgiving
(vi) ending by asking for God's blessing.

*Only one set of prayers is intended to be used each day, at the
time we find easiest.*

One

In the Name of the Father and of the Son and of the
Holy Spirit.

My Lord and my God.

(i)

Glory be to the Father who has made me
Glory be to the Son who has redeemed me
Glory be to the Holy Spirit who gives me life
Praise be to the Holy and undivided Trinity.

(ii)

I am sorry that I have failed to do your will so often,
especially for ... Send your Holy Spirit into my
heart and guard me when I am tempted. Give me
such joy in the triumphant sacrifice of your Son
that it may overflow into the hearts and lives of all
whom I meet.

(iii)

Bless all who need your help: those who are in pain;
the homeless; those suffering injustice and those
tempted to do evil; the worried; those who are
lonely and in despair and all those who care for
them.
Bless all whom I love ... and those whom I dislike
... Guard them and watch over them today and
always.

(iv)

Give me, Lord, courage, strength and endurance to
resist evil and to be loving and helpful in all I do.

(v)

Father, I thank you for all you have given me: for
everyone and everything I love: for my freedom to
enjoy and serve you in your world, and to share in
your life.

(vi)

May the Lord bless and keep me and grant me his
peace for ever.

Two

In the Name of the Father and of the Son and of the
Holy Spirit.

Come Holy Spirit fill me with the knowledge of your
presence.

(i)

Praise the Lord, O my soul; while I live will I praise
the Lord. You are my God and I will praise you,
for you are gracious and worthy of praise; your
mercy is without end. Praise the Lord.

(ii)

O God, I believe you are the God of the whole earth
and that in your great love you sent your Son, Jesus
Christ, to become man like us; to show us yourself
and to die on the Cross so that his loving sacrifice
should bring us back to you in love and penitence.
Make me truly sorry that I have offended you by
not doing what I should have done ... and for
doing what I should not have done ... Father, I
am sorry and will try to live as you would wish.

(iii)

I remember before you those who are in need this
day:
    those who have lost ones they loved
    those who are critically or chronically ill
    those in despair
    those who are old and feel unwanted
    those who are suffering in any other way.

Comfort them all, O Lord, with your presence and
send help to each one of them. Give me courage
and wisdom to do what you desire for them.

(iv)

You have created all that is good and lovely in the
world and given us your Son. Help me to remember
your presence with me this day whatever I am
doing, and in all my work know that you are there.
When I do wrong forgive me and help me to start
again; when I desire to love others, fan the spark
of goodwill in me that it may flame into action for
the sake of him who is perfect love, Jesus Christ,
our Lord.

(v)

Father, I thank you for the power of life in the world
For the life of those who are now with you
For the life of the Holy Spirit in the Church
For the holiness I see in others
For the power to live in love and fellowship with you
and with them.

(vi)

The peace of God, which passes all understanding,
keep my heart and mind in the knowledge and love
of God.

Three

In the Name of the Father and of the Son and of the
Holy Spirit.

Most Holy Trinity, One God in Three Persons, you
are always present in love.

(i)

O God, you are above all, no one can conceive your
greatness
Without you man has no life, no reason, no know-
ledge, no desire, nothing.
You are Father, Saviour, Power of life
You are in majesty the highest
Yet you are in the midst of us as one who serves
You are our peace, our power, our holiness, our hope,
our love.

(ii)

Lord, what you have given me to do, I have not done
. . .
Lord, what you have not wanted me to do, I have
done . . .
I am very sorry that I have offended you in these ways
and I will try to put right what can be mended. I
desire to do your will; forgive my weakness and for
the sake of your Son, send your Holy Spirit to guide
me in the right way day by day.

(iii)

Bless all who have to do difficult things at this time;
those who make important decisions on our behalf

and on behalf of their families and themselves. I pray for all people in their work, especially those who have responsibility for others. Also, I remember before you those in trouble of any kind especially . . ., those who are sick, lonely and afraid. Give them wisdom, courage and compassion and grant that they may finally enter into the peace of your heavenly presence.

(*iv*)

Help me to remember that Christ is in me.
Mine is the body by which he acts,
Mine are the eyes, through which Christ is to look with compassion,
Mine are the feet, with which he is to go about doing good,
Mine are the hands with which he is to bless men now.

(*v*)

Father, I thank you for my life, for the happiness which is mine, especially for . . . and above all for your Son given to us in the Holy Eucharist; the gift of grace which is Christ within me, Christ the light of the world and the guardian of all who seek to follow him. Grant that as long as I live I may praise and adore you, O blessed and glorious Trinity of love.

(*vi*)

The Lord himself be my keeper; be my defence on my right hand; preserve me from all evil, and guard

my following in the way from this time forth for
evermore.

Praying round the Clock

On waking

Our Father . . .

I thank you for the rest that I have had. As another day begins, help me to trust in you whatever lies ahead of me in the hours to come.

Grant this day that I may glorify your name in all the work that you have given me to do. Help me to show forth your love in my dealings with those around me.

9.00 am

Father, send your Holy Spirit upon me at this hour as you sent him upon your disciples. Grant that he may remain with me always.

12.00 noon

The Angelus, in honour of the Incarnation

The Angel of the Lord brought tidings to Mary and she conceived by the Holy Ghost.

Hail Mary,
full of grace,
the Lord is with thee.
Blessed art thou among women,
and blessed is the fruit of thy womb, Jesus.
Holy Mary, Mother of God,
pray for us sinners,
now and at the hour of our death.

Behold the handmaid of the Lord;
be it unto me according to thy word.

Hail Mary . . .

And the Word was made flesh
and dwelt among us.

Hail Mary . . .

Pray for us, O holy Mother of God
That we may be made worthy of the promises of
Christ.

We beseech thee, O Lord, pour thy grace into our
hearts; that as we have known the Incarnation of
thy Son Jesus Christ by the message of an angel,
so by his Cross and Passion we may be brought
unto the glory of his Resurrection; through the
same Christ our Lord.

(From Easter to Pentecost:)
Regina Coeli, in honour of the Resurrection and of Mary

Joy to thee, O Queen of Heaven, Alleluia
He whom thou wast meet to bear, Alleluia
As he promised hath arisen, Alleluia
Pour for us to him thy prayer, Alleluia.

Rejoice and be glad, O Virgin Mary, Alleluia
For the Lord hath risen indeed, Alleluia.

O God, who by the Resurrection of thy Son, our Lord
Jesus Christ, hast vouchsafed to give joy to the
whole world: Grant we beseech thee that, with the
help of his mother the Virgin Mary, we may obtain
the joys of everlasting life; through the same Christ
our Lord.

3.00 pm

Jesus, at this hour you died on the Cross for love of
me.
Help me to love like you.

6.00 pm

Father, in the morning, at noon and in the evening
you come to me, wait for me and would bless me
in all I do. Lord, leave me not but stay with me
always.

At sunset

The hymn of the lighting of the lamps

O gladsome Light of the Holy glory
of the immortal Father,
Heavenly, holy, blest,
O Jesu Christ,
being come to the going down of the Sun.
Seeing the evening light,
we hymn the Father,
and the Son,
and the Holy Spirit of God.
Worthy art thou at all times to be hymned
with holy voices
Son of God
which givest life:
therefore the world doth glorify thee.

Night prayers – from Compline

May the Lord Almighty grant us a quiet night and a
   perfect end.

I confess to God Almighty, the Father, the Son and
   the Holy Spirit, and in the presence of the whole
   company of heaven that I have sinned, especially
   today by . . .
   May God have mercy upon me, forgive me my sins
   and bring me to everlasting life.

Either
Before the ending of the day
Creator of the world I pray
That you, with all your love, will keep
Your guard around me while I sleep.

Or
The day you gave, O Lord, is ended
The darkness falls at your behest.
To you our morning prayer ascended
Your praise will sanctify our rest.

Lord, have mercy and hear me.

Behold now, praise the Lord: all you servants of the
    Lord.
You that by night stand in the house of the Lord:
    even in the courts of the house of our God.
Lift up your hands in the sanctuary: and praise the
    Lord.
The Lord that made heaven and earth: give you
    blessing from his holy city.

Psalm 134

I will lie down in peace and take my rest: for the
    Lord will keep me in safety.

Lord have mercy and hear me.

May the God who gives us peace, make us completely
    his and keep our whole being, spirit, soul and body,
    free from all fault at the coming of our Lord Jesus
    Christ.

Into your hands I commend my spirit: for you have
   redeemed me, O Lord God of truth.

Keep me, Lord, as the apple of an eye: hide me under
   the shadow of your wings.

Save us, Lord.

Lord, now let your servant depart in peace: according
   to your word
For my eyes have seen your salvation: which you have
   prepared for the sake of all peoples
As a light to enlighten the gentiles: and as the glory
   of your people Israel.

Nunc dimittis

Save us, Lord, waking and guard us sleeping, that
   awake we may watch with Christ, and asleep we
   may rest in peace.

Our Father . . .

Either
Lighten our darkness, we beseech you, O Lord: and
   by your great mercy defend us from all perils and
   dangers of this night: for the love of your only Son,
   our Saviour, Jesus Christ our Lord.

Or
Visit, we pray, O Lord, this house and drive far from
   it all the snares of the enemy. May your Holy
   Angels dwell in it to keep us in peace and may your
   blessing be with us evermore; through our Lord
   Jesus Christ.

May Almighty God, the Father, the Son and the Holy
   Spirit, bless, preserve and keep us, this night and
   for evermore.

The peace of God, surpassing all we understand, keep
   our hearts and minds in the knowledge and love of
   God and of his Son, Jesus Christ our Lord: and the
   blessing of God Almighty, the Father, the Son and
   the Holy Spirit be among us and remain with us
   always.

Grace at meals

*There are many of these which may be used or you can make
up your own. Here are just two examples:*

Before
For what we are about to receive may the Lord make
   us truly thankful and make us mindful of the needs
   of others.

After
Thanks be to God.

Praying through the Week

The aim of the following prayers is to use what is given to us in the Bible and in the services of the Church to express our response to God's love for us shown in Creation and Redemption. So each day the theme is one that echoes both the biblical story of Creation and also the saving acts of the life of Christ. The pattern of prayer is the same as in the daily prayers, but you may like to use these instead. They start with a theme for the day, so the pattern is

    (i) theme
    (ii) praise
    (iii) penitence
    (iv) intercession
    (v) petition
    (vi) thanksgiving
    (vii) blessing

These prayers are drawn almost entirely from the Bible except for the short verses at the beginning of each day which come from the old hymns for the daily Offices of the Church. If you have a concordance you can find the biblical quotations, though they have sometimes been adapted and modernised. There are also some texts taken from Church liturgies.

Sunday – light

The day of Resurrection

(i)

This day the first of days was made
When God in light the world arrayed,
Or when his Word arose again
And conquering death, gave life to men.

In the beginning God said, 'Let there be light.'
Jesus said, 'I am the light of the world.'
The light shines on in the darkness and the darkness
   has never overcome it.

(ii)

Praise the Lord, O my soul: you deck yourself with
   light as it were with a garment.

Praise to the Lord and Father of our Lord Jesus
   Christ who in his great mercy gave us new birth
   into a living hope by the Resurrection of Jesus
   Christ from the dead, who shines in our hearts to
   give the light of the knowledge of the glory of God.

(iii)

While we walk in the darkness, our words and our
   lives are a lie: but if we walk in the light, then we
   share together a common life, and we are being
   cleansed from every sin by the blood of Jesus.

Give light to them that sit in darkness and in the
   shadow of death: and guide our feet into the way
   of peace.

(*iv*)

O Lord Jesus Christ, deliver the souls of all the
faithful departed: make them, O Lord, to pass from
death to life: let light eternal shine upon them with
the saints, for you are gracious.

(*v*)

In your light, let me see light.

(*vi*)

O give thanks to the Lord for he is gracious: he has
delivered my soul from death and my feet from
falling, that I may walk before God in the light of
life.

(*vii*)

May the God of peace who brought again from the
dead, our Lord Jesus Christ, our Resurrection and
our Life, keep us in his light.

Monday – the heights and the depths

Christ made man for our sake

(*i*)

O boundless wisdom, God most high
O Maker of the earth and sky
Who makes the parted waters flow
In heaven above, on earth below.

The heavens declare the glory of God: and the firmament shows his handiwork.

The child to be born will be called holy, the Son of God.

Unto us a child is born; unto us a Son is given.

I have come down not to do my own will, but the will of him who sent me.

The Word was made flesh and dwelt among us.

(*ii*)

O Lord our Governor, how excellent is your name in all the world: you have set your glory above the heavens.

My soul magnifies the Lord and my spirit rejoices in God my Saviour.

Who, though he was in the likeness of God, emptied himself and was born in the likeness of men and, in obedience, accepted even death.

That at the name of Jesus every knee should bow, in heaven and on earth and under the earth, and every tongue confess that Jesus Christ is Lord, to the glory of God the Father.

(*iii*)

Out of the depths I call to you, Lord, for in you is found forgiveness.

Create in me a clean heart, O God, and put a new spirit within me.

Lord Jesus Christ, have mercy on me.

(iv)

Keep all men from evil and make them of one heart
    and mind that they may be united in Christ to the
    glory of God.

(v)

Give me a faithful spirit, Lord, that I may truly trust
    in you.

(vi)

Thanks be to God for his gift of our Lord Jesus Christ,
    true God and true Man, through whom the
    Kingdom of Heaven has come to this world.

(vii)

May the God who created all things and sent his Son
    to become man for our sakes, preserve us in peace
    in this world and allow us to share in his heavenly
    glory through Jesus Christ, our Lord.

Tuesday – the waters of life

The baptism of our Lord

(i)

Earth's mighty maker, whose command
Raised from the sea the solid land
And drove each billowy wave away
And bade the earth stand firm for aye.

You rule the raging of the sea: you calm the surging waves.

The heavens are yours, the earth is yours: you laid the foundations of the world and all that it contains.

With joy shall we draw water out of the wells of salvation.

And in that day we shall say, 'Praise the Lord, call upon his name.'

Lo a voice from heaven said, 'This is my beloved Son, with whom I am well pleased.'

He will baptise you with water and the Holy Spirit.

(ii)

The sea is his and he made it and his hands prepared the dry land: O come let us worship and fall down and kneel before the Lord our maker.

We praise you, O God, we acknowledge you to be the Lord: all the earth worships you, the Father everlasting.

Blessed be our Lord Jesus Christ for in him we are baptised into his death and rise again to eternal life.

(iii)

Have mercy upon me, Father, for my soul thirsts for you. Forgive my sin for it is great.

Jesus you bore my sins in your body on the Cross. May I die to sin and live to righteousness.

(*iv*)

Help all men, O God, to put off the old nature of
their life and be renewed in the spirit of their minds,
so that they may put on the new nature in true
holiness.

(*v*)

Grant that I may perceive what you have given me
and give me strength to develop it for the good of
the Body of Christ.

(*vi*)

Thanks be to God for calling me to maintain the unity
of the Spirit in the bond of peace; for the one Faith,
the one Lord and one Baptism.

(*vii*)

Grace be with all who love our Lord Jesus Christ
with love undying: may he become in us a well of
water springing up to eternal life.

Wednesday – the glory of the heavens

The glory of God in Jesus

(*i*)

Thou on the fourth day didst reveal
The sun's enkindled flaming wheel,
Didst set the moon her ordered ways
The stars their ever-winding maze.

The heavens have declared his righteousness: and all the people have seen his glory.

You are worthy, my Lord and God, to receive glory and honour and power, for you created all things and by your will they existed and were created.

Jesus was transfigured before them and his garments became glistening white.

This is my beloved Son: listen to him.

(*ii*)

O speak good of the Lord, all creatures of his: praise the Lord, O my soul.

Holy, holy, holy is the Lord God Almighty who was and is and is to come.

Glory to God in the highest and on earth peace to all men.

My Lord Jesus Christ is the Lord of glory.

Heaven and earth cannot contain you, yet, O my God, you dwell in my heart.

(*iii*)

Listen to my prayer and forgive me.

Lord, I am not worthy that you should come to me: speak the word only and I shall be healed.

(*iv*)

O Lord Jesus Christ, you pray for us now and always: may we ever be with you to behold your glory which the Father gave you before the beginning of the world.

Bring all men everywhere to such perfection that they may see your glory and have eternal peace.

(v)

I pray that I may know you.
Grant that I may live to do your will and in the doing
   of it be transfigured into your likeness.

(vi)

Thanks be to God who has spoken to us by his Son,
   heir of all things, through whom he created the
   world: he reflects the glory of God and bears the
   stamp of his nature, upholding the universe by his
   word of power.

(vii)

The God of all grace, who has called us to eternal
   glory in Christ, restore, establish and strengthen us
   this day and always.
May the light of his countenance shine upon us and
   give us peace.

Thursday – abundance of life

The Body and Blood of Christ

(i)

God brought forth in creative might
A twofold life from ocean's night.
First, all that in the deep abides,
Then those that fly above its tides.

He brings food out of the earth and wine that makes
   glad the heart of man.

He rained down manna also upon them to eat and gave them food from heaven.

So man did eat angels' food: for he sent them meat enough.

Jesus said, 'This is my Body; this is my Blood. As often as you eat this bread and drink this cup, you proclaim my death until I come.'

'I am the living bread which came down from heaven; if any man eat of this bread, he shall live for ever.'

The cup of blessing, is it not a sharing in the Blood of Christ? The bread which we break, is it not a sharing in the Body of Christ? Because there is one Bread, we, who are many, are one Body, for we all partake of the one Bread.

(*ii*)

Praise be to the Lord, who has given meat to them that fear him: praise him in remembrance of his marvellous doings.

Praise be to him who gives fodder to the cattle and feeds the young ravens that call upon him.

Behold how joyful and good a thing it is, brethren, to dwell together in unity.

(*iii*)

I have sinned against you and am no more worthy to be called your son.

Yet I know that the forgiving love of Christ has set creation free from the bondage of sin, and nothing can separate us from the love of God which is in Christ Jesus.

(iv)

Grant that all those who call upon the name of the
Lord Jesus Christ, in every place and in every time,
may be drawn together by the Eucharist into the
Body of Christ as fellow-workers for God.

(v)

Grant that in his Body and Blood I may know the
love of Christ which holds all creation in unity; the
love that surpasses knowledge and fills all it touches
with the fullness of God.

(vi)

I thank you, Father, that you created all things and
gave food and drink to men for their enjoyment,
and especially because to us you have granted food
and drink for eternal life in Christ Jesus.

(vii)

The Lord bless this earth with the abundance of his
mercy and satisfy those who hunger and thirst after
righteousness; that they may find it in union with
Christ, thy Son, our Lord who gave himself for us
that we might have life everlasting.

Friday – the making of man

God reconciles the world to himself through the cross of Christ

(i)

Maker of Man, who from thy throne
Dost order all things, God alone,
By whose decree the teeming earth
To animal and man gave birth.

This alone I know, God made man upright and
  simple: his problems are of his own devising.

All we like sheep have gone astray; we have turned
  everyone to his own way.

The Lord has laid on his servant the iniquity of us
  all: for he was despised and rejected by men; a man
  of sorrows and acquainted with grief.
He himself bore our sins in his body on the Cross
  that we might die to sin and live to righteousness;
  by his wounds we are healed.

(ii)

Praise be to God who made man in his own image
  and saw that he was good.

In this latter day we rejoice, for while we were his
  enemies, we were reconciled to God by the death
  of his Son and are saved by his life.
Now the salvation and the power and the kingdom of
  God and the authority of his Christ have come.
  Therefore let us praise him and magnify him for
  ever.

(iii)

What are these wounds in your hands? The wounds
I received in the house of my friends.

I confess my sins to the Lord: I will acknowledge my
unrighteousness for I know that he will forgive the
wickedness of my heart.
Let the words of my mouth and the meditation of my
heart be always acceptable in your sight, O Lord,
my strength and my Redeemer.

(iv)

Grant that Christ's sufferings shall not be in vain and
that repentance and forgiveness of sins shall be
preached in his name to all nations: his followers
being witnesses to these things.

(v)

Jesus said, 'Father, if it be your will, take away this
cup from me; nevertheless not my will but yours
be done.'

Grant that Christ may dwell in my heart by faith,
that I may have the power to understand the love
of God which surpasses knowledge and be filled
with all the fullness of God, that in me his will may
be done.

(vi)

I thank you for my creation, preservation and all the
blessings of this life and above all for the Redemption of the world by our Lord Jesus Christ, for the
means of grace and the hope of glory.

May God the Father continue to bless us, created
   anew in Christ Jesus, to live the good life which
   from the beginning he meant us to live in perfect
   harmony with him and his Creation.

Saturday – on the seventh day God rested

We wait for Christ's Resurrection

(*i*)

In heaven thine endless joys bestow
And grant thy gifts of grace below.
From chains of strife our souls release,
Bind fast the gentle bands of peace.

I will give peace in the land, and you shall lie down,
   and none shall make you afraid.
The Lord shall give strength to his people: the Lord
   shall give his people the blessing of peace.
It is you, Lord, only who makes us dwell in safety.

Jesus said, 'Peace I leave with you; my peace I give
   to you.'
'Let not your hearts be troubled neither let them be
   afraid, for in me you shall have peace.'
The kingdom of God is righteousness and peace and
   joy in the Holy Spirit.

(*ii*)

How beautiful are the feet of those who preach your
   gospel of peace.

Their voice has gone out to the whole earth, and their words to the end of the world.

Blessed be your name for ever.

Praise be to the Lord for John the Forerunner, who went before your Son, who gives light to those who sit in darkness and in the shadow of death and guides our feet into the way of peace.

(iii)

To the Lord our God belongs mercy and forgiveness.
I have rebelled against him, have not obeyed his voice, nor have I walked in the way of his peace.
I am sorry for my faults which are ever before me.

(iv)

May all who are at variance with one another mend their ways, learn to agree with one another and live in peace.

(v)

Grant that I may not be conformed to this world but transformed by the renewal of my mind, that I may know what is the will of God; what is good, acceptable and perfect in his sight.
In Jesus Christ our Lord may I come to the perfect peace of your kingdom.

(vi)

I give thanks to my God, for the Lord has comforted his people and all the ends of the earth shall see the salvation of our God.

Sorrow and sighing shall flee away and peace shall
establish itself in all creation.

(vii)

May God the Father bless us, who created all things
in the beginning.
May the Son bless us, who for our salvation was made
man.
May the Holy Spirit bless us, who rested as a dove
on the Christ in Jordan. May he sanctify us who
brings us through judgement to the perfection of
peace.

Praying through the Year

Modern language is used here but if the more traditional wording is preferred Psalms and Collects can be found in the Book of Common Prayer.

The Annunciation – the very beginning of the Gospel

God was made flesh and dwelt among us

Hail, O Star that pointest
Towards the port of heaven,
Thou to whom as maiden
God for Son was given.

Behold a virgin shall conceive, and bear a son and
  shall call his name Immanuel – God with us.
                                        Isaiah 7:14

He shall dwell with men, and they shall be his people,
  and God himself shall be with them and be their
  God.
                                        Jeremiah 31:33

God has elected and specially chosen her.

Hail Mary, the Lord is with you. You will conceive
in your womb and bear a Son and you shall call
his name Jesus.

The child to be born will be called holy, the Son of
God.

Blessed are you among women and blessed is the fruit
of your womb.

Blessed are you because you have believed that the
Lord's word would be fulfilled in you.

Luke 1:28, 31, 35, 42, 45

We praise you, Lord

Praise the Lord, O my soul; while I live I will praise
the Lord: yea, as long as I have any being, I will
sing praises unto my God.

Psalm 146:1

Come all you nations and worship the Lord, for a
great light has descended upon the earth.

Praise be to God because in Mary he sheds forth
upon the world the light eternal, Jesus Christ our
Lord.

My God, I am sorry that I have rebelled against you.

Each day I try to set myself above my own worth:
each day I want my own way and not yours.

Help me to remember what you have done for me
through your Son and his blessed Mother.

Mother of God pray for me. Jesus heal me.

We ask you, Mary, for your help

O Mary, as you intervened when wine ran short at a
    wedding and asked your Son to perform a miracle,
    intercede for the whole of mankind: you are the
    link between Creator and created; help all who
    believe in your Son to do whatever he tells them.
You stood beneath the Cross of your Son and shared
    his sufferings: help me, O blessed Mother, to share
    the sufferings of others and pray that God's
    compassion may ever be in my heart.
Pray for me, O Mother of God, that I may be worthy
    of the promises of Christ.

We give thanks to God for Mary

On the Cross Jesus said to Mary and his faithful
    disciple 'Woman behold your son; son behold your
    mother', so making Mary the mother of us all.

I thank you Father for her love and for her trust
    in you which made possible the mystery of the
    Incarnation and our redemption in Jesus.

Lord Jesus, grant that we who celebrate the glory of
    your blessed Mother, may be aided by her prayers
    and share her eternal joys with you.

Advent

Preparation for the Second Coming of our Lord, and for Christmas

Come, ring out our joy to the Lord;
hail the rock who saves us.
Let us come before him, giving thanks,
with songs let us hail the Lord.

A mighty God is the Lord,
a great king above all gods.
In his hand are the depths of the earth;
the heights of the mountains are his.
To him belongs the sea, for he made it
and the dry land shaped by his hands.

Come in; let us bow and bend low;
let us kneel before the God who made us,
for he is our God and we
the people who belong to his pasture,
the flock that is led by his hand.

Psalm 95:1–7

Almighty God, give us grace to cast away the works
of darkness and to put on the armour of light now
in the time of this earthly life, in which your Son
Jesus Christ came to us in great humility: so that
in the last day when he shall come again in his
glorious majesty to judge the living and the dead
we may rise again in his Kingdom of light; who is
alive, and reigns with you and the Holy Spirit one
God now and for ever.

Christmas

The birth of Jesus

Sing a new song to the Lord
for he has worked wonders.
His right hand and his holy arm
have brought salvation.

The Lord has made known his salvation;
has shown his justice to the nations.
He has remembered his truth and love
for the house of Israel.

All the ends of the earth have seen
the salvation of our God.
Shout to the Lord all the earth,
ring out your joy.

Sing psalms to the Lord with the harp
with the sound of music.
With trumpets and the sound of the horn
acclaim the King, the Lord.

Let the sea and all within it, thunder;
the world and all its peoples.
Let the rivers clap their hands
and the hills ring out their joy

at the presence of the Lord: for he comes,
he comes to rule the earth.
He will rule the world with justice
and the peoples with fairness.

Psalm 98

Almighty God, who wonderfully created us in your
    own image and yet more wonderfully restored us

through your Son Jesus Christ: grant, that as he
came to share in our humanity, so we may share
the life of his divinity: who is alive and reigns with
you and the Holy Spirit, one God, now and for
ever.

Almighty God and heavenly King, who sent your Son
into the world to take our nature upon him and to
be born of a pure virgin: grant, that as we are born
again in him, so he may continually dwell in us
and reign on earth as he reigns in heaven with you
and the Holy Spirit now and for ever.

Epiphany

The gentiles come to worship Jesus

The heavens proclaim the glory of God
and the firmament shows forth the work of his hands.
Day unto day takes up the story
and night unto night makes known the message.

No speech, no word, no voice is heard
yet their span extends through all the earth,
their words to the utmost bounds of the world.

There he has placed a tent for the sun:
it comes forth like a bridegroom coming from his tent,
rejoices like a champion to run its course.

At the end of the sky is the rising of the sun;
to the furthest end of the sky is its course.
There is nothing concealed from its burning heat.

Psalm 19:1–7

Heavenly Father, whose blessed Son was revealed
    that he might destroy the works of the devil and
    make us the sons of God and heirs of eternal life:
    grant that we, having this hope, may purify
    ourselves even as he is pure; that when he shall
    appear in power and great glory we may be made
    like him in his eternal and glorious kingdom; where
    he is alive and reigns with you and the Holy Spirit,
    one God, now and for ever.

Almighty God, by whose word and wisdom the bril-
    liant constellations declare your glory, and who led
    the wise men by the light of a star to your infant
    Son, to worship in him the glory of the Word made
    flesh: guide by your truth the nations of the earth
    that the whole world may be filled with your glory;
    through Jesus Christ our Lord.

Epiphanytide

The love of God is shed abroad

My soul, give thanks to the Lord,
all my being, bless his holy name.
My soul, give thanks to the Lord
and never forget all his blessings.

The Lord is compassion and love,
slow to anger and rich in mercy.
His wrath will come to an end;
he will not be angry for ever.
He does not treat us according to our sins
nor repay us according to our faults.

But the love of the Lord is everlasting
upon those who hold him in fear;
his justice reaches out to children's children
when they keep his covenant in truth,
when they keep his will in their mind.

Psalm 103:1, 2, 8–10, 17, 18

Lord, who has taught us that anything we do without
love is worthless: Pour into our hearts that most
excellent gift of love, the true bond of peace and
source of all virtues without which whoever lives is
counted dead before you: Grant this for the sake of
your only Son Jesus Christ; who is alive, and reigns
with you and the Holy Spirit, one God, now and
for ever.

Ash Wednesday

The day of penitence

Have mercy on me, God, in your kindness.
In your compassion blot out my offence.
O wash me more and more from my guilt
and cleanse me from my sin.

My offences truly I know them;
my sin is always before me.
Against you, you alone, have I sinned;
what is evil in your sight I have done.

A pure heart create for me, O God,
put a steadfast spirit within me.
Do not cast me away from your presence,
nor deprive me of your holy spirit.

O rescue me, God, my helper,
and my tongue shall ring out your goodness.
O Lord, open my lips
and my mouth shall declare your praise.

Psalm 51:3–6, 12, 13, 16, 17

Almighty and everlasting God, you hate nothing that
   you have made and forgive the sins of all those
   who are penitent. Create and make in us new and
   contrite hearts, that, lamenting our sins and
   acknowledging our wretchedness, we may receive
   from you, the God of all mercy, perfect forgiveness
   and peace; through Jesus Christ our Lord.

Lent

Preparation for Holy Week

Like the deer that yearns
for running streams,
so my soul is yearning
for you, my God.

My soul is thirsting for God,
the God of my life;
when can I enter and see
the face of God?

My tears have become my bread,
by night, by day,
as I hear it said all the day long:
'Where is your God?'

These things will I remember
as I pour out my soul:
how I would lead the rejoicing crowd
into the house of God,
amid cries of gladness and thanksgiving,
the throng wild with joy.

Why are you cast down, my soul,
why groan within me?
Hope in God; I will praise him still,
my saviour and my God.

Psalm 42:2–6

Merciful Lord, grant to your faithful people pardon
and peace: that we may be cleansed from all our
sins and serve you with a quiet mind; through Jesus
Christ, our Lord.

Holy Week

PALM SUNDAY
Jesus enters Jerusalem

All peoples, clap your hands,
cry to God with shouts of joy!
For the Lord, the Most High, we must fear,
great king over all the earth.

He subdues peoples under us
and nations under our feet.
Our inheritance, our glory, is from him,
given to Jacob out of love.

God goes up with shouts of joy;
the Lord ascends with trumpet blast.
Sing praise for God, sing praise,
sing praise to our king, sing praise.

Psalm 47:2–7

Almighty Father, whose Son was revealed in glory
    before he suffered on the Cross: grant that in seeing
    his divine majesty with the eye of faith, we may be
    strengthened to follow him and through death may
    share his glory; through Jesus Christ our Lord.

MAUNDY THURSDAY
*Jesus gives us the Eucharist and commands us to love each
other*

The Lord is my shepherd;
there is nothing I shall want.
Fresh and green are the pastures
where he gives me repose.
Near restful waters he leads me,
to revive my drooping spirit.

He guides me along the right path;
he is true to his name.
If I should walk in the valley of darkness
no evil would I fear.
You are there with your crook and your staff;
with these you give me comfort.

You have prepared a banquet for me
in the sight of my foes.
My head you have anointed with oil;
my cup is overflowing.

Surely goodness and kindness shall follow me
all the days of my life.
In the Lord's own house shall I dwell
for ever and ever.

Psalm 23

Almighty God, whose Son, the Lord Jesus Christ,
gave us the wonderful sacrament of his Body and
Blood to represent his death and to celebrate his
Resurrection: Strengthen our devotion to him in
these holy mysteries and through them renew our
unity with him and with one another, that we may
grow in grace and in the knowledge of our
salvation; through Jesus Christ our Lord.

GOOD FRIDAY
Jesus dies for us

My heart is stricken within me,
death's terror is on me,
trembling and fear fall upon me
and horror overwhelms me.

If this had been done by an enemy
I could bear his taunts.
If a rival had risen against me,
I could hide from him.

But it is you, my own companion,
my intimate friend!
We walked together in harmony
in the house of God.

O Lord, I will trust in you.

Psalm 55:5, 6, 13–15, 24

Almighty Father hear our prayer and look with favour
   on this your family for which our Lord Jesus Christ
   was ready to be betrayed into the hands of sinful
   men and to suffer death on the Cross; who is alive,
   and reigns with you and the Holy Spirit one God,
   now and for ever.

Easter

Alleluia. Christ is risen

Christians to the Paschal Victim offer your thankful
   praises.
The Lamb the sheep redeems: Christ, by sin unde-
   filed, reconciles sinners to the Father.
Death and life joined together in that conflict stupen-
   dous: the King of life who died deathless reigns.
Declare to us, Mary, the vision of your journey.
'I saw the Tomb of Christ living: and likewise the
   glory of the Risen:
Bright Angels attesting, the shroud and napkin
   resting.
Yea, Christ my hope is arisen: to Galilee he now goes
   before you.'
Christ indeed from death is risen, so we know most
   surely: O King and Conqueror, grant to us mercy.
   Amen. Alleluia.

Lord of all life and power, who through the mighty
   Resurrection of your Son has overcome the old
   order of sin and death and has made all things new
   in him: Grant that being dead to sin and alive to
   you in union with Christ Jesus we may live and

reign with him in glory; to whom with you and the
Holy Spirit be praise and honour, glory and might
now, and in all eternity.

Ascension

Jesus reigns

Alleluia.

Praise, O servants of the Lord,
praise the name of the Lord!
May the name of the Lord be blessed
both now and for evermore!
From the rising of the sun to its setting
praised be the name of the Lord!

High above all nations is the Lord,
above the heavens his glory.
Who is like the Lord, our God,
who has risen on high to his throne
yet stoops from the heights to look down,
to look down upon heaven and earth?

Psalm 113:1–6

Sovereign Lord of the Universe whose Son our
Saviour Jesus Christ ascended in triumph to rule
in love and glory over all creation: As in our flesh
Christ reigns supreme so may all that you have
made obey his will, and all mankind acknowledge
the authority of his kingdom now, and in its
glorious fulfilment when you, our Lord and God,
will be all in all.

Pentecost

The coming of the Holy Spirit

I will hear what the Lord God has to say,
a voice that speaks of peace,
peace for his people and his friends
and those who turn to him in their hearts.
His help is near for those who fear him
and his glory will dwell in our land.

Mercy and faithfulness have met;
justice and peace have embraced.
Faithfulness shall spring from the earth
and justice look down from heaven.

The Lord will make us prosper
and our earth shall yield its fruit.
Justice shall march before him
and peace shall follow his steps.

Psalm 85:9–14

Almighty God, who on the day of Pentecost sent the
   disciples the gift of your Spirit, filling them with
   joy and power and with boldness for Christ: Give
   us this same power and send us out as witnesses to
   the wonder of your love; through Jesus Christ our
   Saviour who with you and the Holy Spirit rules
   over all creation, now and for ever.

Trinity

God in three persons

O send forth your light and your truth;
let these be my guide.
Let them bring me to your holy mountain
to the place where you dwell.

And I will come to the altar of God,
the God of my joy.
My redeemer, I will thank you on the harp,
O God, my God.

Why are you cast down, my soul,
why groan within me?
Hope in God; I will praise him still,
my saviour and my God.

Psalm 43:3–5

Lord of all time and space by whose inspiration we
have been led to acknowledge the glory of the
eternal Trinity, and in the power of whose divine
majesty we worship the unity: Keep us steadfast in
this faith that we may be united in your boundless
love; through Jesus Christ your Son our Lord, who
with you and the Holy Spirit is alive, and reigns in
the unity of perfect love supreme over all things,
God, for ever and ever.

Cry out with joy to the Lord, all the earth.
Serve the Lord with gladness.
Come before him, singing for joy.

Know that he, the Lord, is God.
He made us, we belong to him,
we are his people, the sheep of his flock.

Go within his gates, giving thanks.
Enter his courts with songs of praise.
Give thanks to him and bless his name.

Indeed, how good is the Lord,
eternal his merciful love.
He is faithful from age to age.

Psalm 100

Merciful God, who has prepared for those who love
   you such good things as pass man's understanding:
   inspire us with such love for you that loving you in
   and above all we may obtain your promises which
   exceed all that we can desire; through Jesus Christ
   our Lord.

Feasts of Our Lady

You are the fairest of the children of men
and graciousness is poured upon your lips:
because God has blessed you for evermore.

Therefore God, your God, has anointed you
with the oil of gladness above other kings:
your robes are fragrant with aloes and myrrh.

From the ivory palace you are greeted with music.
The daughters of kings are among your loved ones.
On your right stands the queen in gold of Ophir.

The daughter of the king is clothed with splendour,
her robes embroidered with pearls set in gold.

May this song make your name for ever remembered.
May the peoples praise you from age to age.

Psalm 45:3, 8–10, 14, 18

God, who received into your glory the Blessed Virgin
   Mary, mother of your only Son: Grant that we who
   have been redeemed by his Blood may with her
   share the splendour of your eternal kingdom;
   through Jesus Christ your Son our Lord.

For any Saint's Day

O God, you are my God, for you I long;
for you my soul is thirsting.
My body pines for you
like a dry, weary land without water.
So I gaze on you in the sanctuary
to see your strength and your glory.

For your love is better than life,
my lips will speak your praise.
So I will bless you all my life,
in your name I will lift up my hands.
My soul shall be filled as with a banquet,
my mouth shall praise you with joy.

On my bed I remember you.
On you I muse through the night
for you have been my help;
in the shadow of your wings I rejoice.
My soul clings to you;
your right hand holds me fast.

Psalm 63:2–9

Almighty Father, you have built up your Church through the love and devotion of your saints. We give thanks for your servant ... whom we commemorate today. Strengthen us with *his* (*her*) prayers, inspire us by *his* (*her*) life so we may rejoice with *him* (*her*) in the vision of your glory: through Jesus Christ our Lord.

Quick Prayers to be used at any Time

Lord, I believe, help thou my unbelief.

Come to my heart, Lord Jesus, there is room in my heart for you.

My Lord and my God.

Jesus, my Lord, I you adore, O help me love you more and more.

Come, Lord Jesus.

Praise the Lord, O my soul, and all that is within me praise his holy name.

Have mercy upon me, O Lord, after your great goodness.

Thou givest all, thou givest thyself, what can I withhold from thee, my Lord and my God.

Not unto me, O God, not unto me, but unto thee be the praise.

My God and my all.

Lord, make me content to do thy will.

O Lord, thou knowest how busy I must be this day.
  If I forget thee do not thou forget me.

O Lord, thou art my God, early will I seek thee.

O God, thou art with me always, whom then shall I
  fear?

Blessing and glory and wisdom and thanksgiving and
  honour and power and might be unto our God for
  ever and ever.

Jesus mercy, Mary pray.

O Lord, convert the world and begin with me.

*As you get to know the Father better the heart will form its
own words to praise and adore him, so that whatever you are
doing becomes God's work, and the quick prayer to him
becomes part of your continual fellowship with him. If further
inspiration is needed, the Psalms are a constant source which
covers the whole range of human experience and has a word
for every occasion.*

Prayers at the Eucharist

It is as the members of the Church come together in the worship of the Eucharist that they are most perfectly united in Christ. In these actions given us by Jesus himself, we are able to join in the great thanksgiving and praise of God which goes on continually in heaven and on earth. Jesus gave himself in loving sacrifice for all men, so that all his people and all his creation could be made anew as everyone and everything turns back to the Creator whom they had rejected. The material elements used in the Eucharist, of bread and wine, consecrated to become the Body and Blood of Christ, witness to the value of all material things and of all human life.

It is, then, in and through the Eucharist that prayer has its deepest meaning, and as we take part week by week or day by day our own individual prayers deepen, and the acts of praise, penitence, intercession, petition and thanksgiving flow in and out of the public prayers of the Eucharist. The more we pray with others and by ourselves, the more we open up ourselves to Christ that he may work his purpose in us. So let us not divorce one activity from the other but realise fully the opportunities given us that we may more truly unite ourselves to God and to each other to the greater glory of the Father, whose love for us is beyond all human understanding.

Preparation

Before coming to take part in the Eucharist it is usual to prepare ourselves by using some prayers which can be found in other parts of this book. The prayers commonly used by Christians can be said. The section on penance could be used once a week and the daily prayers for Thursday are especially appropriate, or you may like to use the following:

Jesus is the Lamb of God who takes away the sins of the world: happy are those who are called to his supper.

I do not presume
to come to this your table, merciful Lord,
trusting in my own righteousness,
but in your manifold and great mercies.
I am not worthy
so much as to gather up the crumbs under your table.
But you are the same Lord
whose nature is always to have mercy.
Grant me therefore, gracious Lord,
so to eat the flesh of your dear son Jesus Christ
and to drink his blood,
that I may evermore dwell in him,
and he in me.

ASB Rite A (adapted)

Almighty God,
to whom all hearts are open,
all desires known,
and from whom no secrets are hidden:
cleanse the thoughts of my heart
by the inspiration of your Holy Spirit,

that I may perfectly love you,
and worthily magnify your holy name;
through Christ our Lord.

ASB Rite A (adapted)

Lord Jesus, you gave yourself for me: wash me, heal me, strengthen me with your Body and Blood so I may do what you want me to do and be what you want me to be, giving myself to you.

I offer the Holy Sacrifice for . . . (whatever objects or intentions are closest to your heart).

Before the service

Father, I come into your house to worship you: to give you praise with all who are here present; to give myself to you in union with Jesus and to remember before you all those for whom I would pray. Accept this service which I offer with your Church on earth and in heaven and make it perfect through the sacrifice of your Son.

Lord Jesus fill me with your love.
By the mystery of your Body and Blood first given to your disciples on the night before you died; and through your Ascension into the realm of heaven,
Draw me to yourself.

Two things I recognise in myself, Lord:
I am made in your image;
I have defaced that likeness.
I admit to my fault.

Take from me what I have spoiled;
Leave in me what you have made.
                    from *Private Prayers* by Brother Kenneth

At the readings

Lord, be in my heart and in my mind, that I may
    hear and understand your word.

At the prayers for the Church

Father, I pray for those who have asked for my
    prayers and who need them, especially . . .

At the offertory

Blessed are you, Lord, God of all Creation.
Through your goodness we have this bread to offer,
    which earth has given and human hands have
    made.
It will become for us the bread of life.
Blessed be God for ever.
You have wonderfully created man and still more
    wonderfully redeemed him.
Grant as water is mixed with wine and strengthened,
    so our human nature may be enriched by the
    mystery of the divine life of your Son.
Blessed are you, Lord, God of all Creation.
Through your goodness we have this wine to offer,
    fruit of the vine and work of human hands.
It will become our spiritual drink.
Blessed be God for ever.

Lord:
Yours is the greatness, the power and the splendour,
The victory, the majesty, the praise and the glory.
Everything in heaven and in earth is yours
You are exalted over all supreme
You are ruler over all
Yours it is to give power and strength.
May you be blessed Lord God and Father
From of old and for ever and ever.

from Private Prayers

Receive us, Lord God, as we come to you with humble
    and contrite hearts.

May the Lord accept the sacrifice of his priest and
    people to the praise and glory of his name, for our
    good and the good of all his Church.

At the words of institution

Lord Jesus you are here. Come to my heart, Lord
    Jesus, there is room in my heart for you.

Dying you destroyed our death
Rising you restored our life
Lord Jesus, come in glory.

Father, we offer you this life-giving bread, this saving
    cup, the acceptable sacrifice which brings salvation
    to the whole world.

Before Communion

Lord, I am not worthy that you should come to me
  but speak the word only and I shall be healed.
Grant Lord that eating your Flesh and drinking your
  Blood I may dwell in you and you may dwell in
  me for ever.

Lord Jesus Christ, Son of the living God,
by the will of the Father
and the work of the Holy Spirit,
your death brought life to the world.
By your holy body and blood
free me from all my sins and from every evil.
Keep me faithful to your teaching,
and never let me be parted from you.

Roman Missal

At Communion

Soul of Christ sanctify me
Body of Christ save me
Blood of Christ inebriate me
Water from the side of Christ wash me
Passion of Christ strengthen me
O good Jesu hear me
Within thy wounds hide me
Suffer me not to be separated from thee
From the malicious enemy defend me
In the hour of my death call me
And bid me come to thee
That with thy saints I may praise thee
For ever and ever.

My Lord and my God.

After Communion

Lord Jesus Christ, you have given me yourself, grant
that I may be as generous as you. May the power
of your love strengthen me that I may learn to die
to all that is at enmity with you, as you died on
the Cross for love of me. May this your sacrifice
unite all of us here in the bonds of your love, that
together in the power of your Holy Spirit, we may
learn to live in deeper fellowship with one another
and with you.

Father of all, we give you thanks and praise, that
when we were still far off you met us in your Son
and brought us home. Dying and living, he
declared your love, gave us grace, and opened the
gate of glory. May we who share Christ's body live
his risen life; we who drink his cup bring life to
others; we whom the Spirit lights give light to the
world. Keep us firm in the hope you have set before
us, so we and all your children shall be free, and
the whole earth live to praise your name; through
Christ our Lord.

ASB Rite A

*After the priest has left the altar, stay if possible for a few
minutes and think with thanksgiving of God's goodness to you.*

Before leaving

Father, as I leave this holy place I give you thanks
for the great gift of your Son and the knowledge
that through him we can come to know you more
perfectly and join together in his body, the Church,
to worship you.

Now I dedicate myself to you afresh as I go back to
take my place in the world which you have created:
I give you my hands to do your work
I give you my feet to follow Christ
I give you my eyes to see what you see
I give you my tongue to speak your words
I give you my mind that you may think through
me
I give you my spirit that I may ever pray to you
I give you my heart that you may love through me
I give you my whole self that you may grow in me.

Grant that, in the power of your Holy Spirit, I may
always be ready to love, adore and glorify you by
the doing of your will wherever I may be.

Making a
Spiritual Communion

*By sharing the Body and Blood of Christ in Holy Communion
we become more closely united with him and one another;
therefore we should try to do this as often as possible. However,
there are times when we cannot get to church and other times
when we are there but cannot receive our Lord in this way. In
cases such as these we should make a spiritual communion by
means of which we receive the grace which is closely linked
with the Sacrament.*

*If you are unable to get to church you may like to use the
collect, epistle and gospel for the day and pray for some special
need as you unite yourself spiritually with the Church as it
offers its greatest act of worship and thanksgiving.*

Out of the depths I cry to you, O Lord,
Lord, hear my voice!
O let your ears be attentive
to the voice of my pleading.

If you, O Lord, should mark our guilt,
Lord, who would survive?
But with you is found forgiveness:
for this we revere you.

My soul is waiting for the Lord,
I count on his word.
My soul is longing for the Lord

more than watchman for daybreak.
Let the watchman count on daybreak
and Israel on the Lord.

Because with the Lord there is mercy
and fulness of redemption,
Israel indeed he will redeem
from all its iniquity.

Psalm 130

O Lord Jesus Christ, in union with the whole of your
Church as it offers the sacrifice of your Body and
Blood to the Father, I give you praise and thanks-
giving for this most glorious Sacrament of our
Redemption. Together with this I offer my whole
self which longs to be united with you for ever. O
Lord, I beseech you to come into my heart and
give me the grace of your presence within me that
I may come to love you more and more and never
be separated from you.

O all you works of the Lord, O bless the Lord.
To him be highest glory and praise for ever.

And you, angels of the Lord, O bless the Lord.
To him be highest glory and praise for ever.

And you, rivers and seas, O bless the Lord.
And you, creatures of the sea, O bless the Lord.
And you, every bird in the sky, O bless the Lord.
And you, wild beasts and tame, O bless the Lord.
To him be highest glory and praise for ever.

And you, children of men, O bless the Lord.
To him be highest glory and praise for ever.

O Israel, bless the Lord, O bless the Lord.
And you, priests of the Lord, O bless the Lord.
And you, servants of the Lord, O bless the Lord.
To him be highest glory and praise for ever.

And you, spirits and souls of the just, O bless the
Lord.
And you, holy and humble of heart, O bless the Lord.
Ananias, Azarias, Mizael, O bless the Lord.
To him be highest glory and praise for ever.

Let us praise the Father, the Son, and Holy Spirit:
To you be highest glory and praise for ever.
May you be blessed, O Lord, in the heavens.
To you be highest glory and praise for ever.

Canticle of Daniel: 1–2, 10–14 (Grail)

May your blessing be ever with me and keep me close
to you for ever.

A Visit to the Blessed Sacrament

It is good to slip into church for a few minutes when you can to say your prayers. If our Lord is present there in his great Sacrament any of these prayers may be used, or if you can find a hymn book look up one or more of the hymns suggested.

O Lord Jesus, in this wonderful Sacrament you have left us a memorial of your Passion: grant us so to venerate the sacred mysteries of your Body and Blood that we may ever perceive within us the fruit of your redemption; through the power of the Holy Spirit with whom you reign in the glory of the Father, world without end. Amen

The divine praises

Blessed be God
Blessed be his holy name
Blessed be Jesus Christ, true God and true Man
Blessed be the name of Jesus
Blessed be his most Sacred Heart
Blessed be his most Precious Blood
Blessed be Jesus in the most Holy Sacrament of the
 altar
Blessed be the Holy Ghost the Paraclete

Blessed be the great Mother of God, Mary most
  Holy
Blessed be her Holy and Immaculate Conception
Blessed be her glorious Assumption
Blessed be the name of Mary, Virgin and Mother
Blessed be St Joseph, her chaste spouse
Blessed be God in his angels and in his saints.

Hymns which can be used

Laud, O Sion, my salvation

Just as I am, without one plea

Let all mortal flesh keep silence

Wherefore, O Father, we thy humble servants

Lord Jesus Christ, you have come to us

Firmly I believe and truly

These are only examples; there are many other suitable ones.

Act of faith

O most loving Jesus, I believe that you are really
  present in this most Holy Sacrament. Lord I
  believe, help my unbelief.

Act of hope

I hope, O Jesus, by virtue of the sacrifice you made
for me, to overcome all my sins; to persevere in
goodness; to die in grace and to rise again at the
last day.

Act of charity

O Jesus, I want to love you as your Mother and all
the saints do. I long to praise you on this earth
that I may find myself joining with those who
praise you now in heaven.

Act of praise

Unto him who loves us, and washed us from our sins
in his own blood, be glory and dominion for ever
and ever.

Our Lord's teaching on the Eucharist

Jesus said to them, 'I am the bread of life; he who
comes to me shall not hunger, and he who believes
in me shall never thirst.'

'All that the Father gives me will come to me; and
him who comes to me I will not cast out.'

'This is the bread which comes down from heaven,
that a man may eat of it and not die.'

'I am the living bread which came down from heaven; if anyone eats of this bread, he will live for ever; and the bread which I shall give for the life of the world is my flesh.'

John 6:35, 37, 50, 51

Intercessions

God has made the whole earth, and every creature who lives on it belongs to him, so we should remember when we pray that his love and care are for all as ours should be also. Here is a scheme we can follow when praying for others, but it will be too long for most people to use all at once, so be selective and use two or three sections at a time.

For all things

Father I pray for the whole of your creation.
For the seasons of the year, that they may bring
   health
   fruit
   peace to all men.
For everything.

For all mankind

Those who are Christians
Those of other faiths
Atheists and agnostics
Those who do not live in the truth
Those who live evil lives
Those who try to do your will

Those who love
Those who are
   depressed
   sick
   anxious
   weak and unstable.
Those who are
   cheerful
   healthy
   peaceful
   strong in mind.
Those who have died.
For everybody.

For the Church

All members of the churches
   Eastern
   Western
   Our own
   Those who work for unity in the Church
   Those who seek truth for the Church
   Those who live Christian lives
   Bishops and Clergy
   The Laity
   Religious communities
   Missionaries
   The lapsed and the apostate.
For the whole Church of God in Christ Jesus.

For our life in the world

Those in authority everywhere
Our Queen and Royal Family
The Government and Parliament.
For all who rule.

For all who keep the peace

Judges, lawyers, juries
Police and those in the armed services
Prison governors and warders
Administrators and civil servants
Mayors and councils.
For all to whom I owe order and peace.

For industry

Bankers and financiers
Industrial leaders
Trade unionists
Workers in factories
Shopkeepers and assistants
Farmers and all who work on the land
Fishermen
Builders
Those in service industries
All who work with their hands.
For all who supply my needs.

For education

Parents
All educational authorities
Governing bodies
Teachers and pupils
Scientists and researchers
Universities and colleges
Lecturers and students
All who work in adult education
All who work with children.
For all who taught me and teach me.

For those working in the media

Entertainers
Sportsmen and women
Publishers
Workers in television and radio and films
Writers and artists
Musicians.
For all who help to enrich life.

For the caring professions

Surgeons, doctors, psychiatrists, nurses
Ward orderlies, chaplains
Social workers and probation officers
Those who work for charities.
For all who care for my health and well-being.

For those in difficulties

Children at risk
Deprived communities and refugees
Unemployed
Exploited
Homeless and living in bad conditions
Poor and hungry
Sick in mind and body
Divorced and those suffering as a result
Victims of cruelty
Drug addicts and alcoholics
Those who encourage evil and cause suffering
Those attempting to reform
Those who are afraid
The old and lonely.
For all I know who suffer.

For those in conflict with society

Young offenders
Terrorists
Hardened criminals
Those serving life sentences
Those who intend to defy the law
The weak-willed
Those suffering injustice
Political prisoners
Those imprisoned for the Faith.
For those I should help.

For those for whom I should pray

Family, friends and those I love and admire
Godchildren and those whom I should care for
Those who have asked for my prayers
Those who dislike me or I them
Those who have helped me at any time
Those I serve or who serve me
Those I have injured in any way
Those educated by me or with me
Those who work with me
Those who do not pray
Those who have no one to pray for them.
For my relationship with others.

For animals

The happiness of those in my charge
The badly treated
The starving and strayed
Those threatened with extinction.
For my fulfilment of my responsibilities towards those creatures God has placed in my charge.

Remember, O Lord Jesus, all whom I have brought before you in my prayers and all those I have forgotten, for you know all things and the desires of all men.

You are the help of the helpless
The hope of those who hope no longer
The Saviour of those who are in doubt

The harbour of those who travel along the way
The healer of the sick
You are all things to all men, who came into the world that you might bear our griefs and share our joys.

The Lord bless us and keep us
The Lord make his face to shine upon us and be gracious to us
The Lord lift up his countenance upon us and give us peace.

Some Special Prayers:
For all men according to their needs

O God, the Creator and Preserver of all mankind, we humbly beseech you for all sorts and conditions of men; that you would be pleased to make your ways known unto them, your saving health to all nations. More especially we pray for the good estate of the Catholic Church; that it may be so guided and governed by your good spirit, that all who confess and call themselves Christians may be led into the way of truth, and hold the faith in unity of spirit, in the bond of peace and in righteousness of life. Finally we commend to your fatherly goodness all those who are in any way afflicted or distressed in mind, body or estate; that it may please you to comfort and relieve them, according to their several necessities, giving them patience under their sufferings, and a happy issue out of all their afflictions. And this we beg for Jesus Christ, his sake.

For the sick in mind and body

Try to identify yourself in prayer with the sick person through the suffering of Jesus, holding him in our Lord's presence. Pray that he may be supported by the love of Christ whose pain he shares. If you can, let him know that you are praying for him. He may be too distressed to pray himself.

Father, I ask you to comfort those who are sick in mind or body especially . . .
May your Holy Spirit give them
  Strength to bear their pain
  Grace to seek you in their troubles
  Courage to give themselves to you in love
  A willingness to share in the sufferings of Christ
  True healing in this life
  The hope of glorious happiness to come when you restore all things to their first perfection, and the results of evil are done away.

For the dying

Go forth Christian soul from this world in the name of God, the Father Almighty who created you; in the name of Jesus Christ, Son of the living God, who suffered for you; in the name of the Holy Spirit who was poured out upon you; in the name of the angels and archangels and of all the hosts of heaven; in the name of the Patriarchs, Prophets, Apostles, Evangelists, Martyrs, Confessors, Virgins and of all the Saints of God; let the place you inhabit be in peace and your home in the heavenly Jerusalem.

For Christians who have died

O Lord Jesus Christ, the Creator and Redeemer of
all the faithful, grant to the soul of your servant . . .
the forgiveness of all his sins, growth in love of you
and eternal rest with your saints.

Give rest, O Christ, to your servant with your saints:
where sorrow and pain are no more neither sighing,
but life everlasting.
You only are immortal, the Creator and maker of
Man:
And we are mortal, formed of the earth, and to earth
shall we return:
For so you did ordain when you created me, saying
Dust you are, and to dust shall you return.
All we go down to the dust; and weeping at the grave
we make our song:
Alleluia, Alleluia, Alleluia.

For those who have not died in faith

O Father, you have created all men for yourself and
given them the freedom to worship or reject you.
Your mercy far surpasses that of men: we do not
presume to judge those who seem lost on this earth.
Grant to them a chance to realise the truth and to
come to know you and be with you for ever. You
sent your Son to save all men; do not now reject
those who with new knowledge would turn to
worship you, for the sake of Jesus Christ who ever
lives to make intercession for us all.

For those who mourn

O merciful Lord God, you have given us your Son to
bring light to them that sit in darkness and in the
shadow of death: look upon all whose hearts are
troubled by the loss of one whom they loved.
Comfort them and grant them a sure trust and
confidence in your fatherly care and give them
peace of heart in the midst of their sorrow.

Meditation and Contemplation

God calls all people to a loving union with himself. We need to be single-minded to achieve this and so we need a real desire to follow the way God wishes each one of us to go. We can be sure that God will help, guide and support us in learning to love him.

Meditation on the Gospels

Because God is simple we must learn to be simple too if we are to know and love him. This simplicity is shown to us in Jesus Christ, so when we pray we can do no better than meditate on parts of the Gospels which tell us what the early followers of Jesus discovered about him.

It is good to set apart a time to pray in this way, perhaps once a week or at shorter intervals if we can. The time of day depends on the individual; a little experience and advice from a priest or one capable of giving it will soon put this right.

1 Sit or kneel quietly – try to relax and give this time to God.
2 Ask for the help of the Holy Spirit: 'Come Holy Spirit, fill my heart with your presence and pray in me.'

3 Read the piece from the Gospel you have chosen, two or three times.

4 Try to think what it is saying. What is God saying through it? (You may like to picture the scene in your mind, but if you cannot see what it means give it up – don't strain.) You can usually find:

    (a) what its meaning was to the first Christians;

    (b) some phrase which appears important;

    (c) its meaning for you.

5 This may lead you to express your feelings in words and thoughts of love of God and Creation.

6 Whatever sticks in your mind, hold on to it – and think of it during the day.

7 You may wish to thank God for the time you have spent with him by deciding to do some little thing for him during the day.

The real aim of this is to let God's love into us, and it follows that if we do this we shall become better Christians.

Example of a meditation

Read Mark 9:33–7

What does it say?
Jesus asked his disciples what they were discussing.
They were silent because they were ashamed.
They had discussed who was the greatest.
Jesus told his disciples that if anyone wanted to be great in God's eyes he had to serve others.
Jesus took a child and told them that if they received

the child they received him and that meant they received the one who sent him, God himself.

What is God saying through it?
(a) Meaning for first Christians:
The greatness God recognises is not the same as that which men recognise.
(b) Important phrase:
If anyone would be first, he must be last of all and servant of all.
(c) What is this saying to me?
God first, others second, self last.
In everyone I meet, I meet Christ.
I must remember this and treat them with love and courtesy.

Thought for the day
'He who receives me, receives the one who sent me.'

A little thing to do for him
I will let my friend decide what we are to do today instead of expecting him to fall in with my wishes.

This is only one person's framework; for another these words could lead him in quite a different direction, but the goal will be the same, God himself, the source of all things.

The prayer of Jesus

Meditation is simply *a* way of praying and some people cannot do it in *this* way. For them, to repeat a prayer over and over again slowly can have real value. For example, the prayer of Jesus:

Lord Jesus Christ, Son of God,
have mercy on me, a sinner.

The Lord's Prayer said slowly, dwelling on each
phrase, is really a form of meditation and the Rosary
on p. ooo is a good way to dwell on the mysteries of
the Gospel and the Church. Hymns can also be used.

It is possible to meditate on almost anything in
God's world and be led to the Creator, so do not be
wedded to the Bible if suddenly you find it grows
stale on you; branch out into literature, art, music,
or think of some good experience which has happened
to you and in which you can see God's hand. Whatever you choose to do, God is at the end of the line
and he will help you know and love him if that is
your desire.

The prayer of silence

Many great men and women of prayer in East and
West, including non-Christians, have found silence to
be the most effective prayer. There are various ways
to approach God in silence. They usually include
taking up some particular physical position to relax
the tension of the body and using a single repeated
word to relax the tension of the mind (for example,
sitting on the floor or in clear space and in a balanced
posture, breathing quietly and saying the name of
Jesus slowly until self-consciousness disappears). An
alternative way is to think of some very peaceful
scene. After some considerable time – fifteen minutes
at least – a sense of the peace and depth of the mystery
of God and of life may often come. Rest in this.

Afterwards you will be able to see things in perspective and as God wills you to see them.

Retreats

If we want or need to meditate in depth perhaps the best way is to go and spend a few days at a convent or monastery or retreat house. Many parishes have an annual retreat for members of their congregations, where a priest or religious suggests subjects for meditation. Often silence is kept among those on retreat, which can help us to relax and be still with God. Other people find it more valuable to go on retreat by themselves, perhaps asking someone for guidance on what they should read or consider while they are there.

Retreats are particularly valuable to us when we have some important decision to make or when we find it difficult to resolve some inner conflict. Often they can prove to be very enjoyable, a banquet for the spirit. It is a great privilege to be able to drop in to the worship of a religious community and be strengthened by it. And, though a good deal of effort is required to organise oneself to go and make the best use of a retreat, it can certainly be a marvellous holiday from everyday chores and cares.

(And cheap, too!)

Penitence

See Luke 15:11-32: The story of the Prodigal Son.
Father, I have sinned against heaven and before you.

*Every day you will be aware of your failure to live in Christ,
and a few seconds thinking about him will make you conscious
of this; but once a week it should be possible to spend a little
longer trying to see more deeply what this means by using this
scheme of thought.*

Prayer before thinking how you have failed God

O God, I thank you for being so good to me and
especially for sending your Son into the world to
save me from my sins. Send your Holy Spirit into
my heart now and show me how I have failed to
do your will. Give me the grace to be really sorry,
and time to put right what is wrong, for the sake
of Jesus Christ, our Lord.

What is sin?

Sin is a failure in Love. Our Lord said:
You shall love the Lord your God with all your heart,
and with all your soul and with all your mind and
with all your strength and your neighbour as yourself.
Mark 12:29, 30

So when we sin, we sin against:
1 God
2 Others
3 Ourselves

1 Ask yourself what you have
   (a) failed to do for God
       e.g. not praying
   (b) done against your relationship with God
       e.g. not standing up for him.
2 Ask yourself what you have
   (a) failed to do for others
       e.g. neglect of parents or friends
   (b) done against your relationship with others
       e.g. thinking, talking or doing evil to them.
3 Ask yourself what you have
   (a) failed to do for yourself
       e.g. not using the gifts you have
   (b) done against yourself
       e.g. using your gifts wrongly.

Confession – the sacrament of reconciliation

Jesus said to his apostles:
'Peace be with you, as the Father has sent me, even
so I send you.' And when he had said this, he
breathed on them, and said to them, 'Receive the
Holy Spirit. If you forgive the sins of any, they are
forgiven; if you retain the sins of any, they are
retained.'

John 20:21–3

Our Lord has given power to his Church to forgive

sins, and this power is given to every priest at his
ordination and so the Church provides for the person
who may feel he needs to tell what is wrong in his
life to another and to be assured of God's forgiveness.
The priest is the human agent of the Sacrament
through which the grace of forgiveness comes upon
the penitent. If you feel the need to seek forgiveness
in this way, the opportunity is there, and you should
talk to a priest about making your confession before-
hand, so that you truly understand what you are
doing. Anything shared with a priest in these circum-
stances will never be mentioned to you or to another
unless you particularly request it. You may also want
to tell the priest about things which puzzle or worry
you, so that he can give you advice.

After having used the plan of self-examination as
suggested, go to the church at the time arranged. (It
is a good idea to write down your sins on a small
piece of paper before making your confession – but
remember to tear it up afterwards.)

When your turn comes, go to the priest and kneel
down. The priest will give you a blessing. You then
say:

I confess to Almighty God, to all the company of
heaven and to you, Father, that I have sinned in
thought, word and deed, through my own fault
(especially since my last confession which was . . .
ago, I have committed these sins) . . .

[Say simply what you have discovered is wrong
and then conclude:]

For these and all my other sins which I cannot now
remember I am truly sorry, mean to amend my life

and humbly ask pardon of God; and of you, Father, penance, advice and absolution.

The priest may offer advice. He will suggest you do some small penance like saying a psalm or special prayer, and give you absolution. The priest will then give you a blessing and ask you to pray for him, remembering that he is also a sinner like you.

Go back to your place and kneel down: say your penance: thank God for the grace he has given you; resolve to try very hard to live a more loving life in future.

You may find your priest prefers to treat confession informally, to hear your confession in his study or in your home. Sometimes there may be an opportunity given in your parish to come together with others to prepare for confession.

Remember to decide with your priest to make a rule about how often you will seek God's forgiveness in this way. Of course God can forgive sins apart from the confessional but sacramental confession assures us of his forgiveness in a special and authoritative way.

If you decide not to make use of sacramental confession, you are advised to use one of the acts of penitence given in the three sets of daily prayers (pp. 20–6); the one contained in the third set is especially appropriate.

Traditional Prayers

In each section these are arranged in alphabetical order as far as possible.

To God the Father

The General Thanksgiving
Almighty God, Father of all mercies, we thine
   unworthy servants do give thee most humble and
   hearty thanks for all thy goodness and loving kindness to us and to all men.
We bless thee for our creation, preservation and all
   the blessings of this life; but above all for thine
   inestimable love in the Redemption of the world by
   our Lord Jesus Christ, for the means of grace and
   the hope of glory. And we beseech thee, give us
   that due sense of all thy mercies, that our hearts
   may be unfeignedly thankful, and that we show
   forth thy praise, not only with our lips but in our
   lives; by giving up ourselves to thy service, and by
   walking before thee in holiness and righteousness
   all our days; through Jesus Christ our Lord, to
   whom with thee and the Holy Ghost be all honour
   and glory, world without end.   Amen

Almighty God, who seest that we have no power of
   ourselves to help ourselves; keep us both outwardly
   in our bodies, and inwardly in our souls; that we

may be defended from all adversities which may
happen to the body, and from all evil thoughts
which may assault and hurt the soul; through Jesus
Christ our Lord.

Be present, O merciful God, and protect us through
the silent hours of this night, so that we who are
wearied by the changes and chances of this fleeting
world may rest upon thy eternal changelessness;
through Jesus Christ our Lord.

Bless all who worship thee, from the rising of the sun
unto the going down of the same. Of thy goodness
give us; with thy love inspire us; by thy spirit guide
us; by thy power protect us; in thy mercy, receive
us now and always.

Defend us, O Lord, with thy heavenly grace, that we
may continue thine for ever, and daily increase in
thy Holy Spirit more and more, until we come to
thine everlasting kingdom.

God be in my head and in my understanding
God be in mine eyes and in my looking
God be in my mouth and in my speaking
God be in my heart and in my thinking
God be at mine end and at my departing.

God, who didst teach the hearts of thy faithful people
by the sending to them the light of thy Holy Spirit,
grant us by the same Spirit to have a right judgement in all things, and evermore to rejoice in his
holy comfort; through the merits of Christ Jesus
our Saviour, who liveth and reigneth with thee, in

the unity of the same Spirit, One God, world without end.

Grant to us, O Lord, to know that which is worth knowing; to love that which is worth loving; to do that which pleaseth thee most, to esteem that which is most precious unto thee, and to dislike whatsoever is evil in thine eyes. Grant us with true judgement to distinguish things that differ, and above all to search out and to do what is well-pleasing unto thee, through Jesus Christ.

Lighten our darkness, we beseech thee, O Lord; and by thy great mercy defend us from all perils and dangers of this night; for the love of thy only Son, our Saviour, Jesus Christ.

Lord, make me an instrument of your peace
Where there is hatred, let me sow love
Where there is injury, pardon
Where there is doubt, faith
Where there is despair, hope
Where there is darkness, light
Where there is sadness, joy.
O Divine Master
Grant that I may not so much seek to be consoled as to console
To be understood as to understand
To be loved as to love.
For it is in giving that we receive
It is in pardoning that we are pardoned
It is in dying that we are born to eternal life.

Make what is true more true to me, let fuller light
    appear
All that is evil, take from me, all that is doubtful,
    clear.
Let no false confidence betray, no foolish fears mislead
But in the right and narrow way, be thou my hope
    indeed.
Do more for me than I can know; from self my will
    set free
Thy perfect gift of love bestow, that I thy child may
    be.

O God, forasmuch as without thee we are not able to
    please thee; mercifully grant that thy Holy Spirit
    may in all things direct and rule our hearts, through
    Jesus Christ our Lord.

O God, of thy goodness
Give us thyself,
For only in thee
Have we all.

O Lord, our God, grant us grace to desire thee with
    our whole heart; so that, so desiring, we may seek,
    and seeking, find thee; and so finding thee, may
    love thee, and loving thee, may hate those sins from
    which thou hast redeemed us.

O Lord, support us all the day long, till the shades
    lengthen and the evening comes, and the busy
    world is hushed, and the fever of life is over and
    our work is done. Then in thy mercy, grant us a
    safe lodging, a holy rest and peace at the last.

Prevent us, O Lord, in all our doings with thy most gracious favour, and further us with thy continual help; that in all our works begun, continued and ended in thee, we may glorify thy holy name, and finally by thy mercy obtain everlasting life; through Jesus Christ.

Take us, we pray thee, O Lord of our life, into thy keeping this night and for ever; O thou, Light of lights, keep us from inward darkness; grant us so to sleep in peace, that we may arise to work according to thy will; through Jesus Christ our Lord.

Teach us, good Lord, to serve thee as thou deservest; to give and not to count the cost; to fight and not to heed the wounds; to toil and not to seek for rest; to labour and not to ask for any reward, save that of knowing that we do thy will, through Jesus Christ our Lord.

Visit we beseech thee, O Lord, this dwelling and drive far from it all the snares of the enemy. Let thy holy Angels dwell herein to preserve us in peace, and may thy blessing be upon us evermore.

Te Deum Laudamus
We praise thee, O God: we acknowledge thee to be the Lord.
All the earth doth worship thee: the Father everlasting.
To thee all angels cry aloud: the heavens and all the powers therein.

To thee Cherubim and Seraphim: continually do cry,
Holy, Holy, Holy: Lord God of Sabaoth;
Heaven and earth are full of the Majesty: of thy glory.

The glorious company of the Apostles: praise thee.
The goodly fellowship of the Prophets: praise thee.
The noble army of Martyrs: praise thee.
The Holy Church throughout all the world: doth
  acknowledge thee;
The Father of an Infinite Majesty;
Thine honourable, true: and only Son;
Also the Holy Ghost: the Comforter.

Thou art the King of Glory: O Christ.
Thou art the everlasting Son: of the Father.
When thou tookest upon thee to deliver man: thou
  didst not abhor the Virgin's womb.
When thou hadst overcome the sharpness of death:
  thou didst open the Kingdom of Heaven to all
  believers.
Thou sittest at the right hand of God: in the glory of
  the Father.
We believe that thou shalt come: to be our Judge.
We therefore pray thee, help thy servants: whom thou
  hast redeemed with thy precious Blood.
Make them to be numbered with thy saints: in glory
  everlasting.

O Lord, save thy people: and bless thine heritage.
Govern them: and lift them up for ever.
Day by day: we magnify thee;
And we worship thy name: ever world without end.
O Lord, have mercy upon us: have mercy upon us.
O Lord, let thy mercy lighten upon us: as our trust
  is in thee.

O Lord, in thee have I trusted: let me never be confounded.

To our Lord Jesus Christ

O Lord Jesus Christ, Son of the living God, who at the evening hour didst rest in the sepulchre, and didst thereby sanctify the grave to be a bed of hope to thy people; make us so to abound in sorrow for our sins, which were the cause of thy passion, that when our bodies lie in the dust our souls may live with thee, who livest and reignest with the Father and the Holy Spirit ever one God, world without end.

O Lord Jesus Christ, take and receive all my liberty
My memory, my understanding and all my will: all I have and possess.
Thou hast given it: to thee, O Lord, I return it.
All is thine: dispose of it according to thy will.
Give me thy love and grace, for that is enough for me.

O Lord Jesus Christ, who didst say to thine Apostles: Peace I leave with you, my peace I give unto you: regard not our sins, but the faith of thy Church, and grant it that peace and unity which is according to thy will.

O Saviour of the world, who by thy Cross and precious blood has redeemed us; save us and help us we humbly beseech thee, O Lord.

Thanks be to thee, O Lord Jesus Christ, for all the benefits which thou hast given us; for all the pains and insults which thou hast borne for us. O most merciful Redeemer, friend and brother, may we know thee more clearly, love thee more dearly and follow thee more nearly, for thine own sake.

Watch thou, dear Lord, with those who wake or watch or weep tonight, and give thine angels charge over those who sleep. Tend thy sick ones, Lord Christ; rest thy weary ones; bless thy dying ones; soothe thy suffering ones; shield thy joyous ones and all for thy love's sake.

The Great Advent Antiphons

O Sapientia
O Wisdom, which camest out of the mouth of the most high, and reachest from one end to another, mightily and sweetly ordering all things: Come and teach us the way of prudence.

O Adonai
O Adonai, and leader of the House of Israel, who appearedst in the bush to Moses in a flame of fire, and gavest him the law in Sinai: Come and deliver us with an outstretched arm.

O Radix Jesse
O Root of Jesse, which standest for an ensign of the people, at whom kings shall shut their mouths, to whom the gentiles shall seek: Come and deliver us, and tarry not.

O Clavis David

O Key of David, and Sceptre of the house of Israel; that openest and no man shutteth, and shuttest and no man openeth: Come and bring the prisoner out of the prison house, and him that sitteth in darkness and the shadow of death.

O Oriens

O Dayspring, brightness of light everlasting and Sun of Righteousness: Come and enlighten him that sitteth in darkness and the shadow of death.

O Rex Gentium

O King of the nations and their desire; the Cornerstone, who makest both one: Come and save mankind whom thou formedst of clay.

O Emmanuel

O Emmanuel, our King and Lawgiver, the desire of all the nations and their salvation: Come and save us, O Lord our God.

O Virgo Virginum

O Virgin of Virgins, how shall this be? For neither before thee was any like thee, not shall there be after. Daughters of Jerusalem, why marvel ye at me? The thing which ye behold is a divine mystery.

To God the Holy Spirit

Come Holy Spirit, fill the hearts of thy faithful people and kindle in them the fire of thy love.

Come Holy Ghost, our souls inspire
And lighten with celestial fire

Thou the anointing Spirit art
Who dost thy sevenfold gifts impart:

Thy blessed unction from above
Is comfort, life and fire of love
Enable with perpetual light
The dullness of our blinded sight:

Anoint and cheer our soiled face
With the abundance of thy grace
Keep far our foes, give peace at home
Where thou art guide no ill can come.

Teach us to know the Father, Son
And thee, of both, to be but One,
That through the ages all along
This may be our endless song:

Praise to thy eternal merit,
Father, Son and Holy Spirit.

Come, O Holy Spirit, come, Spirit of holy fear, banish
from our hearts all other fears but one, the fear of
grieving thee.

Come, O Holy Spirit, come to us, O thou Spirit of
Wisdom, that we may be filled with the wisdom of
the wise. Come, O Holy Spirit, come to us,
enlighten   our   hearts   with   the   spirit   of
understanding.

Pentecost Sequence

Come thou Holy Paraclete
And from thy celestial seat
Send thy light and brilliancy.

Father of the poor draw near
Giver of all gifts be here
Come the soul's true radiancy;

Come of comforters the best
Of the soul the sweetest guest
Come in toil refreshingly.

Thou in labour rest most sweet
Thou art shadow from the heat
Comfort in adversity;

O thou light most pure and blest
Shine within the inmost breast
Of thy faithful company.

Where thou art not, man hath nought
Every holy deed and thought
Comes from thy divinity;

What is soilèd make thou pure
What is wounded work its cure
What is parched fructify.

What is rigid gently bend
What is frozen, warmly tend
Strengthen what goes erringly.

Fill thy faithful who confide
In thy power to guard and guide
With thy sevenfold mystery.

Here thy grace and virtue send
Grant salvation in the end,
And in heaven, felicity.   Amen   Alleluia

Holy Spirit, instruct us how to fulfil our vocations:
    teach us to finish the work our heavenly Father has

given us to do: show us how to bend our wills to
the will of God, how to conform our lives to the
pattern of the life of Christ; that living, we may live
to him, and dying, we may die to him and rising,
we may wake up after his likeness and be satisfied
for ever and ever.

O Holy Spirit, the Comforter, we worship thee, very
God, equal to the Father and the Son, bond of the
everlasting Godhead. We worship thee, proceeding
from the Father and the Son – the spring of all
creation – the source of all life. We adore thee,
breathing into man the breath of life. We adore
thee, causing thy light and life to shine in the darkness of our hearts, and we praise thee for ever.

O Holy Spirit, thou Lord and giver of life, we adore
thee in the everlasting being of thy unchangeable
majesty. Teach us to know that in thee we live, by
thee we move, by thee we have our being.

We beseech thee, Blessed Spirit, to light up in our
hearts that fire which our Lord Jesus Christ came
to send on earth.

With thy bright flame our senses light, into our hearts
thy true love pour, thy people once again unite, the
glory of thy Church restore.

To the Trinity

To God the Father who loves us and makes us
accepted in the beloved

To God the Son, who loves us and loosed us from
our sins by his own blood

To God the Holy Spirit who sheds the love of God
abroad in our hearts

To the one true God be all love and all glory for time
and for eternity.

Some Contemporary Prayers

All powerful Father guard me
Eternal Son guide me
Life giving Spirit govern me.
Make my prayers right and my thoughts good; forgive
   what offended you in the past, put right what is
   wrong now
Lead me from sin in the future.
                    from *Private Prayers* by Brother Kenneth

Eternal God
   You are the power behind all things:
   Behind the energy of the atom
   Behind the heat of a million suns.
Eternal God
   You are the power behind all minds:
   Behind the ability to think and reason
   Behind all understanding of the truth.
Eternal God
   You are the power behind the Cross of Christ:
   Behind the weakness, the torture and the death
   Behind unconquerable love.
Eternal God
   We worship and adore you.
                    from *Contemporary Prayers* by Caryl Micklem

Father in heaven, you have given us a mind to know

you, a will to serve you and a heart to love you.
Be with us in all that we do, so that your light may
shine out in our lives.

from *A Christian's Prayer Book*

God, I love you above everything else and for no
other reason except you, yourself.
I want you.
I long for you.
Always in all things, with all my heart and being I
look for you.

from *Private Prayers*

Grant us this day, O God
Peace with you,
that the certainty that you love us may take all fear
away,
that we may know
that your love has forgiven us,
that your grace upholds us,
that your welcome awaits us.

from *Prayers for the Christian Year*
by William Barclay

Holy Spirit:
Don't let it ever be completely true that I couldn't
care less.
Take from me all pride, envy, anger, greed, lust,
laziness and an uncontrollable desire to possess
people and things.
Help me to wrap myself in humility and love, patience
and self-control.
Make me pure and content with what I have, serving
with unflagging energy.

I rely on your unfailing love now and for evermore.

from *Private Prayers*

Holy Spirit:

Let there be a harvest in me of love, joy, peace, patience, kindness, gentleness and self-control.

Spirit of wisdom and insight, counsel and power, knowledge and fear of God, live in me.

from *Private Prayers*

It's no good; I'm empty; I'm bored; I don't really believe.

So if you are there, do something please.

from *It's me, O Lord*
by M. Hollings and E. Gullick

Lord:

be within me to give me strength

over me to protect me

beneath me to support me

in front of me to be my guide

behind me to prevent me falling away

surrounding me to give me courage.

from *Private Prayers*

Lord Christ, crucified for us,

help us to love, as you have loved

help us to live, as you have lived

help us to be neighbours to our fellow man in his need as you in your mercy were neighbour to us and suffered and died for us.

In your name we ask it.

from *Contemporary Prayers*

Lord God:
May I adore you with reverence
Put nothing or no one in your place
Neither misuse your name
Nor be ashamed to admit my allegiance to you.
Make me kind and affectionate, patient and gentle
Help me to enjoy my body in purity
Give me honesty and contentment
Destroying in me all unreal fantasies
Jealous hope and shameful thoughts.

from *Private Prayers*

Lord, I thank you for the peace you give us when we let go our worrying, forget our self-concern, cease our rushing about, and rest in you. This wonderful peace fills the whole of me and overflows into the world. It makes me love you and those around me in an all-embracing way. Lord, help me to be self-forgetting and never let me try to possess this peace for myself, for, like your love, it must be continually outgoing.

from *It's me, O Lord*

Lord Jesus, you were tired, but were you ever too tired to care?
Lord I am so tired that I can hardly keep going. Give me strength to keep on peacefully so that I do not snap at the people about me. Give me your kind of strength which in weariness still thinks of others, and when night comes give me peaceful rest in sleep, and I'll try again tomorrow.

from *It's me, O Lord*

Lord you know what is right for me
You want what is good for me
You can do what is best for me
I can neither know nor do what is good
I don't even want it as I should.
In your immeasurable goodness and love make me
  what is best for you and therefore what is best for
  me.

from *Private Prayers*

O come, Holy Spirit, inflame my heart, set it on fire
  with love.
Burn away my self-centredness so that I can love
  unselfishly.
Breathe your life-giving breath into my soul so that
  I can live freely and joyously. Come like a gentle
  breeze and give me your still peace so that I may
  be quiet and know the wonder of your presence in
  my being and help diffuse it in the world. Act freely
  in me and through me, and never leave me, O Lord
  and giver of life.

from *It's me, O Lord*

O God, our Father, we come to you
  Not because we are strong, but because we are
  weak
  Not because we have any merits of our own but
  because we need mercy and help.
Grant unto us this day the mercy and the pity which
  are yours.

from *Prayers for the Christian Year*

O God, grant to us this day moments of silence,
   periods of inner stillness so we may be taken hold
   of by those realities which words cannot convey.

                              from *Prayers of Hope*

O loving Father grant
That guided by your light we may reach the light
   that never fades
That illumined by your truth we may reach the truth
   which is complete
That in the end we may see light in your light and
   know even as also we are known.

                    from *Prayers for the Christian Year*

Show us, good Lord,
   the peace we should seek
   the peace we must give
   the peace we can keep
   the peace we must forgo
   and the peace you have given in Jesus our Lord.

                          from *Contemporary Prayers*

Thank you good Lord, for the experience of being
   alive.
For being able to feel, think, choose and love.
Thank you for the new delights and opportunities
   which this day brings.

                              from *Prayers of Hope*

The Rosary

In religious bookshops you may have seen rosaries for sale. They are a circular string of beads with a pendant of five beads and a crucifix. To pray using beads is not only an ancient Christian practice: we share it with Muslims and Buddhists. For prayer is a matter for the body as well as for the mind and spirit. The idea is that as we move our fingers over the beads we say prayers we know by heart and while we say the prayers we think not of the prayers but of the meditations (called 'mysteries') of events in the lives of Jesus and Mary which are described below. As we go on, the movement of our fingers stills the fidgetiness of our bodies and the automatic saying of the prayers quietens our minds so that they are free to think about the mysteries. This may sound very complicated but is in fact one of the easiest ways of meditating, being drawn through the eyes of Mary to see Jesus more clearly and love him more dearly.

How to say the Rosary
Begin by holding the Crucifix at the end of the tail and say the Apostles' Creed (p. 18), the summary of our Christian faith. Then hold the first bead between finger and thumb and say an Our Father thinking of the intention for which you are praying – e.g. for someone who needs your prayers. Then move on, holding the next bead and saying the Hail Mary (p. 17) on that, and the following two beads in praise of

the Father, who made Mary, the Son, who redeemed her, and the Holy Spirit, who gave her the fullness of grace. On the fifth bead say the Glory be (p. 18). All this helps to take us into the stillness of prayer.

Now start on the circle. Say the Our Father holding on to the medallion, a Hail Mary on each of the ten beads of the decade as it slips through your fingers and a Glory be on the last and separate bead. Throughout all this you meditate on the mystery chosen. You have now completed one decade.

Start the next by saying the Our Father on that same separate bead and then carry on through the next ten beads etc. as before, meditating on the next mystery. And go on until you have finished the circle of the five mysteries. End up with the final prayers on p. 129.

When you get in the way of saying the Rosary, you will find it is very easy to use, perhaps just a decade at a time, when you are on the bus or underground or while you are kept waiting for something. It is also good to say a decade on arriving in church before a service to recall the presence of God. The Rosary may sound like 'vain repetition' but it really is not. Use only one set of mysteries at a time. You can always count on your fingers instead of using the beads if you do not want to be noticed.

The five joyful mysteries

1 *The Annunciation*
When the angel comes to Mary, God's love for us all is brought to a single focus in her: she is asked

to be the mother of Christ. In saying 'yes' to God
she brings the Saviour of us all into the world.

Luke 1:26–38

2 *The Visitation*
Mary, now pregnant, goes out of love and kindness
to visit her cousin Elizabeth, soon to become the
mother of St John the Baptist. They greet each
other rejoicing in wonder at God's grace to them
in the child Mary is to bear.   *Luke 1:39–56*

3 *The Nativity*
Jesus is born, the Son of Mary and the Son of God,
in the stable at Bethlehem. The shepherds in their
simplicity, the wise men in their wisdom, share in
her adoration of the Child. She cares for him with
a mother's tenderness.

Luke 2:1–20; Matt. 2:1–12

4 *The Presentation in the Temple*
Joseph and Mary bring the baby Jesus to his
heavenly Father's house for the first time and,
following the Jewish law, offer a sacrifice to ransom
the child who will offer his life as a ransom for all
men. With the insight of the old, Simeon and Anna
recognise him as the light of the world and Mary
treasures their words.   *Luke 2:22–38*

5 *The Finding of the Child Jesus in the Temple*
Jesus has grown to the age when he knows that he
must put God first, so he stays in the Temple when
Joseph and Mary leave for Nazareth. They turn
back to find him and their sorrow is turned to joy
when at last he is found.   *Luke 2:41–52*

The five sorrowful mysteries

1 *The Agony in the Garden*
Jesus prays in a sweat of fear as he waits to be betrayed, while his friends sleep. Yet his trust in his Father is so great that he can still say, 'Thy will be done'.   *Mark 14:32–50; Luke 22:39–46*

2 *The Scourging at the Pillar*
The flesh of Jesus is torn by the whips of human hatred. The punishment due to evil is exacted from the innocent: yet by his suffering we are healed.
Matt. 27:11–26

3 *The Crowning with Thorns*
The cruel crown is forced on Jesus' head in mockery. He is truly King of Kings and in silence suffers the scorn of humanity.   *Matt. 27:27–31*

4 *The Carrying of the Cross*
Jesus, both priest and victim, bears the weight of the Cross on which he is to be sacrificed to make good all the weight of evil in the world he has come to save.   *Mark 15:21, 22*

5 *The Crucifixion and Death of our Lord*
Jesus is nailed to the Cross and lifted up to die in pain and loneliness. He hangs there in darkness until, as he dies, he knows that he has done what he came to do: now his sacrifice of love is perfect and complete.   *Luke 23:32–47*

The five glorious mysteries

1 The Resurrection
Jesus lives! The tomb is empty: he is seen by Mary
Magdalene and the disciples. Christ enters his
Kingdom of eternal life, the first of a great multi-
tude. He goes with his friends on their journey and
is known in the breaking of the bread.
Matt. 28:1–10; Luke 24:13–35

2 The Ascension
Christ the King goes to his Father in heaven, gives
authority to his Apostles for the task of spreading
the Kingdom and promises to be with us all until
the end of time, until we are all joined in him.
Acts 1:1–11; Matt. 28:16–20

3 The Descent of the Holy Spirit
on Our Lady and the Apostles
On Mary and the Apostles as they pray at Pentecost, the Holy Spirit descends like fire to illuminate
their minds and inspire their hearts with courage
for their vocation to be Christ's Body in his world.
Acts 2:1–13

4 The Assumption
Mary, the Mother of Christ and so the Mother of
all Christians, her life's work over on earth, dies
and is taken into heaven to pray and care for us
all.
Luke 1:42–9

5 *The Coronation of Our Lady as Queen of Heaven*
All the saints rejoice in Jesus, our Lord and our
God. He, too, delights in them, above all in his
Mother, Mary. She is the Queen of heaven. They
are united in his glory.   *Rev. 12:1–6*

Prayers after the Rosary

Hail, holy Queen, Mother of mercy. Hail, our life,
our sweetness and our hope. To you we cry, poor
exiled children of Eve; to you we send up our sighs,
mourning and weeping in this vale of tears. Turn,
then, most gracious advocate, your eyes of mercy
towards us. And after this our exile, show us the
blessed fruit of your womb, Jesus. O gentle, O
loving, O sweet Virgin Mary.

Queen of the most holy Rosary, pray for us, that we
may be made worthy of the promises of Christ.

O God, whose only-begotten Son, by his life, death
and resurrection, has opened for us the rewards of
eternal life, grant that meditating on these
mysteries in the most holy Rosary of the Blessed
Virgin Mary, we may both imitate what they
contain, and obtain what they promise, through
Christ our Lord.

Stations of the Cross

This is a set of prayers usually associated with Lent and Holy Week, when we think particularly of the suffering of our Lord. There are often in churches carvings or pictures, or just numbers beneath a cross, which indicate the stations, from the Judgement Hall of Pilate to the Holy Sepulchre, which the pilgrims to the Holy Land would observe in Jerusalem at sites traditionally associated with them. By following in our imagination our Lord's path of pain and death as we go round the church, we bring ourselves closer to him and to the love and sorrow of his mother as she watched him die.

Before we start it is good to think of some particular person (or people) who is suffering so that we can make this devotion in trust that God will make their sufferings fruitful for good and joy as those of Jesus were.

The prayers which follow are an adaptation of the prayers associated with the congregational form of stations.

In front of the altar
Jesus, my saviour, see me kneeling before you, praying for all who suffer especially . . . , for myself and for all who need your grace. Grant us all salvation through the infinite merits of your passion on which I am to meditate. May my heart be so moved to sorrow and repentance as I follow the

path of your pain that I may be ready to meet with joy the sufferings and humiliations of my pilgrimage on earth.

Before each station
We adore you, O Christ, and we bless you: because by your holy Cross you have redeemed the world.

Then say a prayer such as the one given after each of the stations, and then say one or more of the following:

O my God, because you are so good, I am very sorry that I have sinned against you, and I will try not to sin again.

Our Father.   Hail Mary.   Glory be.

Lord, have mercy upon us.

Have mercy upon us.

May the souls of the faithful, through the mercy of God, rest in peace.   Amen

After each station a verse of the hymn 'Stabat Mater' may be said, as if we see the sufferings of our Lord in the company of his mother.

I *Jesus Christ is condemned to death*
Jesus, you were innocent yet you consented to suffer for me. I am guilty: bring me to hate my sins and accept your forgiveness.

II *Jesus receives the Cross*
Jesus, grant me by the power of your Cross cheer-

fully to face the trials of my calling as a Christian
and to be ready to take up my cross and follow
you.

III *Jesus falls the first time*
Jesus, you carried the weight of my sins with
your Cross. May the thought of your burden
make me watchful and save me from sin.

IV *Jesus is met by his Mother*
Jesus, you felt grief at your Mother's sorrow: have
mercy on me and ask her to pray for me. Mary,
sorrowful Mother, pray for me.

V *The Cross is laid on Simon of Cyrene*
Lord Jesus, make me willing to bear my cross
with you: may I not shrink from suffering but be
glad to be given the chance of sharing your
calling to suffer.

VI *The face of Jesus is wiped by Veronica*
Jesus, as I see your suffering, may I desire more
and more to love you, to comfort you and serve
you.

VII *Jesus falls a second time under the Cross*
Jesus, falling again under the weight of my sin,
how often have I hurt you. Make me ready to
bear anything rather than grieve you again.

VIII *The women of Jerusalem mourn for our Lord*
Loving Saviour, I mourn for the pain you endure
because of the evil I have done. Make me hate
all that is evil.

IX *Jesus falls a third time under the Cross*
Jesus, by this third most painful fall pardon my most frequent falls into sin: may the thought of your sufferings make me more faithful.

X *Jesus is stripped of his garments*
Lord Jesus, strip me, I pray, of all pretence, conceit and pride and give me such humility in this life that I may reign with you for ever.

XI *Jesus is nailed to the Cross*
Jesus, you are nailed to the Cross: fasten my heart there also, that sharing in your grief I may come to see your glory.

XII *Jesus dies upon the Cross*
Lord Jesus, dying on the Cross, I worship you. In your death I trust and hope for grace here and for joy in heaven.

XIII *Jesus is laid in the arms of his Mother*
Mary, Mother of Jesus, you bear in your arms your only Son, put to death for my sin. Pray for me that when I come to die, he may take me into his arms for ever.

XIV *Jesus is laid in the sepulchre*
Lord Jesus, your body rests in the grave. Give me grace that I may keep my body in temperance, soberness and chastity; so, when you come to judge the world, it may be renewed in the glory of your Resurrection. Grant that I, having followed your way of sorrows, may be ready to meet you when you call me to you.

Prayer at the altar after the last station

Christ for us became obedient unto death: even the death of the Cross.

Almighty God, we pray you graciously to look upon us, your family, for whom our Lord Jesus Christ was willing to be betrayed and given up into the hands of wicked men and to suffer death upon the Cross; who now lives and reigns with you in the unity of the Spirit for ever and ever.

May the divine assistance remain with us always.

A Final Word

Because each of us is unique no two persons can pray alike; with the help of the Holy Spirit each must find his own way to the Father. So a book such as this cannot teach one to pray; it can only help. We can learn to pray only by praying, just as we learn, as children, to walk by stumbling and falling over many times in the process. Our life of prayer can be like this and, although we may start out with great enthusiasm and a real desire to get to know our Creator better, there will be times when things are hard and to pray becomes a burden unwillingly borne. In days gone by, stern books would have told us to continue our efforts and take no note of our feelings, but our feelings are a very important part of us and we are not right to ignore them in the part of our life which should hold things in perfect balance: our relationship with God. When we feel like this there is a root cause and it is sometimes difficult for us to discover what this is for ourselves. A friend may help, but the right person is not always available, so do not hesitate to go and talk to a priest of the Church or one experienced in the life of prayer about your own problems. They are there to help and even if they cannot advise you personally, they will tell you where to go for aid.

Under ordinary conditions it can be very useful to have a rule of prayer: it is often wise again to discuss this with your priest. We are creatures of habit and prayer is a good habit. Do not be too ambitious in your rule. It is better to have a very easy rule and pray more, than to try to impose on yourself a hard rule and fail: for when we make a promise to God and break it, like Adam and Eve we tend to keep out of his way in future. If you decide to make a rule, write it down on the blank pages at the end of this book, try it out, and if it does not work for you, change it.

In a short book on prayer there are bound to be many things left out. One of the most important is that, though this book begins with George Herbert's poem 'Love', there is almost no poetry apart from the psalms in it. Yet poetry can be full of inspiration for prayer especially at times of depression and dryness. The English language is particularly rich in marvellous poetry which can be used in prayer: some of this is directly religious, like many of the poems of George Herbert, John Donne, Richard Crashaw and, more recently, of William Blake, Gerard Manley Hopkins, T. S. Eliot, R. S. Thomas, Edwin Muir and Charles Causley. There are many anthologies which can be useful and poetry not directly concerned with religion or Christianity can also help to arouse the sense of depth and beauty which leads in to prayer, as indeed

> . . . the meanest flower that blows can give
> Thoughts that do often lie too deep for tears.

One final thing which may be of help. It is often very difficult to settle down to pray: we seem to be pulled away from God back into our everyday interests and anxieties. As you begin to say your prayers, first think of those people who have loved you and who have died and are with God, so that you are surrounded by friends close to him. If there are any saints whom you particularly like, think of them too. Ask them all to help you to pray.

We should like to think that these few pages will serve the purpose of guiding and enabling those who read them to make full use of the ways God has opened to himself through his Son, our Lord Jesus Christ, that each of us may be united to Him and to one another in the Eternal Love of the Trinity.

Acknowledgements

The compilers are grateful to the following for permission to use copyright material: Geoffrey Chapman Publishers, from *A Christian Prayer Book*; the Revd Richard Harries, from *Prayers of Hope* (BBC Publications); Hodder and Stoughton Ltd, from *Private Prayers* by Brother Kenneth; Mayhew-McCrimmon Ltd, from *It's me, O Lord* by Michael Hollings and Etta Gullick; SCM Press Ltd, from *Prayers for the Christian Year* by William Barclay and from *Contemporary Prayers for Public Worship* by Caryl Micklem; A. P. Watt Ltd on behalf of The Grail, England, from the Psalms and the Canticle of Daniel.

Extracts from *The Alternative Service Book 1980*, which is copyright © The Central Board of Finance of the Church of England, are reproduced with permission.

Excerpts from the English translation of *The Roman Missal* © 1973, International Committee on English in the Liturgy, Inc. All rights reserved.

Note

Almost all the quotations from the Psalms are taken from The Grail translation and follow The Grail verse numbering. The numbering of the Psalms themselves, however, follows the numbering in the Bible.

For your own Prayers